THE ORCHARD BOOK OF
SWORDS
SORCERERS &
SUPERHEROES

TONY BRADMAN & TONY ROSS

ORCHARD BOOKS

CONTENTS

THE ORCHARD BOOK OF
SWORDS
SORCERERS &
SUPERHEROES

For Inspector Coffey...
We think the world of you!

T.B.

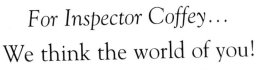

ORCHARD BOOKS
338 Euston Road, London NW1 3BH
Orchard Books Australia
Level 17/207 Kent Street, Sydney, NSW 2000
First published in 2003 by Orchard Books
First published in paperback in 2010
Text © Tony Bradman 2003
Illustrations © Tony Ross 2003
The rights of Tony Bradman to be identified as the author and
of Tony Ross to be identified as the illustrator of this work
have been asserted by them in accordance with the
Copyright, Designs and Patents Act, 1988.
A CIP catalogue record for this book is available from the British Library
ISBN 978 1 40830 921 6
1 3 5 7 9 10 8 6 4 2
Printed in Malaysia
Orchard Books is a division of Hachette Children's Books,
an Hachette UK company.
www.hachette.co.uk

VOYAGE TO THE EDGE OF THE WORLD
THE STORY OF JASON & THE GOLDEN FLEECE

FOR A BOY FROM A ROYAL FAMILY, Jason had a pretty tough start in life. He was born a prince, the son of Aeson, the king of a Greek city. Aeson, however, had a brother, an evil, cunning man called Pelias, who rebelled against him. Pelias threw Aeson into prison, then sent his men to murder the baby Jason. But Jason's mother smuggled her son to safety, and Jason grew to be a fine young man, determined to put right the wrongs Pelias had done.

So one day Jason set out for his home city. As soon as he arrived there, he went straight to the royal palace and demanded a meeting with his uncle.

The guards took Jason to Pelias, who sat on the throne he had stolen from Jason's father.

"How nice to see you, Nephew," Pelias said. "Although somehow I have a feeling you're not just here for a family visit. What can I do for you?"

"You can free my father and give him back his kingdom," said Jason, proudly. "And if you do it now, I will ask him to spare your miserable life."

"Brave words," said Pelias, laughing. "I could have you killed on the spot – but wait, I've got a better idea. I'll do what you want…on one condition."

"Name it," said Jason quickly. "I hereby swear I'll accept whatever it is."

"Very well," said Pelias, grinning at his guards. "I will gladly free your father and make him king again – if you bring me the Golden Fleece."

The guards howled with laughter, and Jason realised he'd been tricked. It was an impossible task. Many had gone in search of the Golden Fleece, and none had returned. But Jason had sworn, and wouldn't go back on his word.

"Is that all, Uncle?" he said. "I was expecting something much harder."

Then he strode from the palace, the guards' jeering ringing in his ears.

But Jason was a lot less confident than he'd sounded. He wasn't even sure where the Golden Fleece was, although legend said it was across the sea.

So Jason went to Argus, the best shipbuilder in Greece, and asked for his help.

Argus built Jason a beautiful ship with a tall mast and fifty oars, and Jason called it the Argo. Then Jason let it be known he was going on a voyage of adventure, and needed a crew of heroes to accompany him. They came from far and wide, the greatest warriors of their time. They called themselves the Argonauts – which is Greek for 'the crew of the Argo' – and soon set sail. They travelled far, and saw many wonders. They survived storms and treacherous seas, they passed safely through the famous Clashing Rocks, they fought savage tribes and monsters, and they grew to be more than just the crew of a ship – they became a true band of brothers. And Jason asked everyone they encountered where the Golden Fleece might be found.

But it was only when they met King Phineas that Jason had any luck.

King Phineas had been cursed by the gods, so every time he sat down to eat a meal, he was tormented by Harpies, foul flying demons, who stole his food. Jason and the Argonauts walked into Phineas' palace one day, just as this was happening. Jason whipped out his sword and rushed forward.

"With me, men!" he yelled, and a furious battle began.

The air was filled with terrifying shrieks as Jason and his men threw their spears, and slashed at the Harpies with their swords, or shot them down with arrows. And the Harpies fought back, beating at the Argonauts with huge wings and raking the men's shields and helmets with razor-sharp claws.

But the Argonauts won in the end, killing most of the Harpies and driving off the remainder. Phineas was overjoyed, and couldn't thank Jason enough.

"There must be something I can do for you in return!" Phineas said at last.

"You could tell us where to find the Golden Fleece," Jason said, putting his sword back in its sheath. "If you know, that is. Nobody seems to."

"I do know," said Phineas, the blood draining from his face. "But I wish you'd asked me anything else. To seek the Golden Fleece is certain death."

"The only thing that's certain," said Jason, "is that I must fulfil my quest."

Phineas was even more impressed by Jason now. So he told him that the Golden Fleece belonged to King Aeetes of Colchis, and how to get there.

It turned out that Colchis wasn't far from Phineas' kingdom. So Jason and the Argonauts bade Phineas farewell, and a few days later they rowed into the harbour at Colchis. It was a grim, forbidding city beneath an iron grey sky. Soldiers lined the harbour walls, silently watching the Argo approach.

The Argonauts tied up at the quayside, and Jason went with some of his men to call on King Aeetes, leaving the rest to keep watch on the ship.

"Greetings, stranger," said King Aeetes, his voice cold, his face hard and unwelcoming. A large bodyguard of fierce-looking warriors was drawn up behind his throne. "Perhaps you would like to tell us what brings you here."

"I've come to ask for your Golden Fleece," Jason replied, deciding it was best to be honest. He noticed there were some other people looking on from behind the bodyguards, among them a dark-eyed young girl who was staring intently at him. "I need it to free my father and restore his kingdom," he said.

"Now why am I not surprised?" Aeetes muttered, giving Jason a thin smile. "You're not the first young hero who's come seeking my Fleece, and I'll tell you what I've told all the others…it's yours, my boy. I will gladly hand it over to you – so long as you perform a couple of small tasks for me first."

"And what might those be?" Jason asked, warily.

"Why, nothing too difficult," Aeetes replied, giving Jason a brief flash of his cold, thin smile again. "Just a bit of ploughing, and sowing some seeds."

Jason felt sure Aeetes was plotting something, but he decided to go along with it for the time being. So he agreed, and Aeetes said he could perform the tasks the next day. Then he invited Jason and all his men to a great feast.

Jason sat next to Aeetes, but noticed the dark-eyed girl staring at him once more. He found out her name was Medea, and that she was the king's daughter. And he also discovered that he couldn't help staring at her, too.

At last the feast was over, and Jason and his men rose from the table to return to the Argo. But as Jason left the palace, someone tugged at his arm.

It was Medea, and she signalled for him to follow her to a dark corner.

"Here, you'll need this tomorrow," she whispered, handing him a small jar of ointment. "Be sure to smear yourself with it before you start ploughing. Then listen out for me to tell you what to do once you've sown the seeds."

"But why do I need this?" Jason asked. "And why are you helping me?"

Medea just kissed him, then slipped away. She loved her father, but as soon as she had seen Jason, she knew she loved him more. Jason thought it was all very strange, but he had fallen in love with her too. So, in the morning, he covered himself with the ointment before he and his men set off for the palace. Aeetes was waiting with his bodyguard at the gates, and led Jason and his men to a field nearby. There was a large barn to one side.

Jason spotted Medea among the other onlookers, and she nodded to him.

"Let's get started," Aeetes said. "Bring out the bulls for the ploughing."

Suddenly the barn door flew open and two enormous, fire-breathing bulls came thundering towards Jason. But Medea's ointment protected him from their scorching flames. He got the bulls harnessed, and ploughed the field.

The Argonauts cheered their leader, but Aeetes frowned at Jason.

"The job's not done yet," said Aeetes. "Here are the seeds to sow."

Aeetes gave Jason a helmet full of what looked like sharp teeth.

Jason shrugged, and walked up and down the furrows he'd ploughed, casting the teeth to right and left. Little did he know that they were dragon's teeth.

And to his horror, from each tooth there sprang a fully armed man. Soon Jason and his men were in a pitched battle, fighting desperately to save their lives. Then Jason heard Medea's voice above the clang of sword on shield.

"Throw the helmet at them!" she yelled. "The one the seeds came in!"

Jason did what he was told – and the instant the helmet landed amongst the warriors, they turned on each other. Within minutes they were all dead.

"I've performed the tasks you set me," Jason said angrily, striding up to Aeetes. "Now keep your part of the bargain – give me the Golden Fleece."

"Of course," said Aeetes, and smiled. "You'll find it in my garden."

Jason told his men to wait while he went into the palace garden. It was a strange, dark, overgrown place with an evil atmosphere. Jason shivered, and nearly jumped out of his skin, when Medea suddenly appeared beside him.

"Sssh…" she hissed at him. "We must be careful not to wake the dragon."

Medea led Jason to the heart of the garden, where a tall oak tree stood. Jason stopped in his tracks, filled with wonder – for there, hanging from one of the tree's branches, was the Golden Fleece. It shone with a magical glow, and was even more amazing than Jason had ever imagined it would be. He could hardly believe that this fabulous prize – something so many other men had died seeking – was at long last almost within his grasp.

But a huge dragon was curled before the tree, and Jason realised now why Aeetes had smiled – Aeetes thought Jason would never get past the Fleece's guardian. However, Medea had given the creature a drug to make it sleep.

Jason crept up and pulled down the Fleece. But the branch snapped as he did so, and fell across the dragon's scaly snout. Jason backed away, holding the Fleece – and his breath.

The dragon slowly opened one eye, then the other. It looked at Jason…then leapt to its feet, roaring with fury.

"Run, Medea!" Jason yelled. He drew his sword and slashed at the great beast as it reared above him, then he turned and ran out of the garden too.

Aeetes was puzzled when he saw his daughter running past him – and furious when he saw Jason appear with the Fleece tucked under his arm.

"Kill the strangers!" Aeetes cried, and his bodyguard moved forward.

But just then the dragon burst out of the garden, roaring and breathing fire and stamping on anyone in its way. The palace and many of the nearby houses went up in flames. Aeetes' men panicked, and Jason saw his chance.

"Quick, men!" he called out above the din. "Back to the Argo!"

And so the Argonauts made their escape. Soon they were rowing away from Colchis as fast as they could, a tall, black cloud of smoke rising behind them. Medea stood close by Jason in the stern, knowing she would probably never see her father again. But she had made her choice, and she was happy.

Jason was happy too. He held the shimmering Fleece in his hands and smiled. He had Medea with him, and the Argonauts, his band of brothers. He couldn't wait to get back, to free his father and banish Pelias forever.

The Argo moved swiftly homewards over the dark sea, towards the setting sun.

THE MAGICAL SWORD
THE STORY OF KING ARTHUR'S BEGINNINGS

LONG AGO, WHEN BRITAIN WAS IN A DARK AGE of war and famine, a young boy called Arthur lived far in the west with his father, Sir Ector, and his big brother, Kay. Sir Ector was a chieftain, and they had a fine castle, so they were safe, and they had plenty to eat. But Arthur knew that times were hard for others.

Kay was nearly a man, had his own warhorse, weapons and armour. Arthur longed for the day when he too would be able to ride a warhorse like Kay's, and have a shield and a great sword at his side. Kay knew that, and loved to tease his little brother and laugh at him.

Then, one cold and misty winter's morning, a messenger rode into Sir Ector's castle. He said there was to be a great meeting of Britain's warlords and chieftains, and that Sir Ector was invited to come. Sir Ector said he would be there, so the messenger galloped off to spread his news elsewhere.

"I hope you'll be taking me with you, Father," said an excited Kay.

"Yes, of course," said Sir Ector. "You'd better come too, Arthur."

Arthur hadn't expected that, so he was surprised and very pleased.

"But why, Father?" said Kay. "He's a boy, and this is man's work!"

"He'll be a man soon enough," Sir Ector said, glancing at Arthur, "and this will help him learn what that means. Besides, you'll need a squire, Kay."

As Kay's squire, Arthur would have to look after his brother's weapons and armour, but he didn't mind that. And Kay seemed to like the idea of being able to give his brother orders, so he didn't complain any more.

A week later, Sir Ector rode off with Kay, Arthur and a small band of warriors. The meeting was to be held in London, the old Roman capital on the opposite side of the country, and a long journey lay ahead of them.

Arthur had never been away from home before. At first he was as excited as Kay, both of them eager to see new sights.

But the further they travelled east, the worse things looked. They passed through burnt fields and villages and towns, and wherever they went the people were hungry and scared.

"This is awful, Father," Arthur said eventually. Kay was riding with the warriors, but Arthur was beside Sir Ector. Arthur was very upset by what he was seeing. It was like riding through some kind of terrible nightmare, he thought. "I don't understand," he said. "Why are things so bad everywhere?"

"It started when the Romans left us to defend ourselves," Sir Ector said quietly, his face grim. "The Saxons invaded, and they've been spreading from the east like a plague ever since, killing our people and taking the land. And the warlords make it worse by squabbling and fighting with each other."

"Why don't they join together to fight the Saxons?" said Arthur.

"Because none of them trust any of the others," said Sir Ector. "And no one has been strong enough to make them listen to reason, not since the days of the last king, the great Uther Pendragon. But even he couldn't keep them under his control for long enough to sweep the Saxons from our shores."

"What happened to him, Father?" Arthur asked. "Did he die in battle?"

"No, Arthur," said Sir Ector quietly, turning towards him as he spoke. Arthur could see Sir Ector had a strange look on his face. "It's thought that some of the warlords plotted against him, and that he was poisoned along with all his family. But nobody has ever really known the whole truth…"

They rode in silence after that, Arthur thinking deeply. He wished that he could do something to help. But what power did he have? He was only a boy, still too young to achieve anything in the hard world of men and war.

"So who has called this meeting, Father?" Arthur asked after a while.

"I don't know," said Sir Ector. "But I do know this might well be our last chance to save ourselves. Although I doubt that the warlords will agree…"

Then Kay came riding up, and Arthur asked no more questions.

A few days later they arrived at the gates of London, and entered the city. Most of the old Roman buildings were ruined, and the streets were crowded with hard, tough men – the warlords of Britain and their followers – their eyes cold, their faces scarred from battle. Distrust hung over the city like a fog.

"Wait here while we find out what's happening, Arthur," said Sir Ector.

Then Sir Ector strode off with his warriors and Kay, leaving Arthur to guard the horses. Arthur noticed Kay's sword hanging from his saddle.

Suddenly Arthur was distracted from his watching by the sound of loud, angry voices. He left the horses to see what was going on, and a tall, dark figure in a hooded cloak brushed by him as he did so, seeming almost to glide over the cobbles like a ghost. Arthur stopped and shivered, the little hairs on the back of his neck standing on end as he watched the figure slip away. Then he shook his head to clear it, and carried on in the same direction he'd been going in before.

Two warriors had been arguing, but by the time Arthur reached them, they had settled their differences and moved off. Arthur quickly returned to the horses, suddenly feeling worried. One look told him Kay's sword wasn't hanging from his saddle any more. Just then Kay himself appeared, alone. "Father sent me back for my sword," Kay said. "Where is it?"

"I don't know…" Arthur said. "I…I think it's been stolen."

"Well, it's your fault," Kay snarled at him. "You're my squire, and you were supposed to be looking after it! So you'd better find me another sword – and be quick about it, or I'll have to tell Father just how useless you are."

Arthur ran from his brother. Night was falling, and Arthur wandered the gloomy, ruined streets of London. Men were clustering for warmth now round their campfires. Arthur wondered how he could have been so stupid – and where he could possibly find another sword to replace the one that he had lost.

Then he bumped into that tall, dark, hooded figure for a second time.

"You may find what you seek in there," said the hooded man, and pointed beyond him. Arthur looked, and saw a large pavilion in a nearby courtyard.

When he turned round again, the hooded man had vanished into the darkness! It seemed even stranger than before, but though the hairs on the back of his neck stood up again, Arthur didn't stop to think about it.

He slipped into the pavilion. It contained a block of stone surrounded by tall candles that cast a golden glow. There was some writing carved on the stone, which Arthur ignored. He was too busy looking at the sword sticking into it. Arthur grabbed the hilt and pulled, and the sword came out smoothly. A tingle shot up his arm, but Arthur ignored that too, and went to find Kay.

"Now that's what I call a sword," said Kay, grabbing it without thanks.

Arthur hadn't noticed quite how good a sword it was, with its jewelled pommel and its fine steel blade that seemed to catch the light, any light. But when the boys found their father, Sir Ector noticed the sword immediately.

"That's not your sword, Kay," he said. Sir Ector wanted to know what had happened to Kay's own sword, and where he'd got the other. Kay blustered, claiming he'd swapped his old sword for the new one. Sir Ector obviously didn't believe a word of it, and Arthur finally told their father the truth.

"Take me to this stone, Arthur," said Sir Ector. "I want to see it."

Arthur did as he was ordered.

The three of them went through the dark streets to the courtyard, and the pavilion was the same as when Arthur had left it, the block of stone standing inside, the candles still burning, no one else there. But now Sir Ector stood in front of it and read the carved writing aloud. "He who draws the sword from the stone is the true-born King of Britain."

"Arthur was lying, Father," said Kay, quickly stepping forward. "He didn't pull the sword from the stone – it was me! So I must be the true-born king."

"Well then, it should be easy for you to perform this miracle once more, my son," said Sir Ector. "Put the sword back in the stone and pull it out."

Kay placed the tip of the sword on the stone, and it slid in up to the hilt with a clang. Then Kay pulled...and nothing happened. He pulled till his face was red and he groaned, but the sword wouldn't move. Then Sir Ector tried, using all his strength, and still the sword stayed stuck in the stone.

"Now you try, Arthur," Sir Ector said at last.

Arthur gripped the hilt in a daze, gave the gentlest of tugs – and the sword came out smoothly. Arthur felt that tingle in his arm again, but far more powerfully. He stared at the sword, spellbound by its beauty. Then he saw that his father and brother were kneeling before him, their heads bowed.

"But why are you kneeling before me?" Arthur said. "I…I can't be king…"

"Ah, but you can, Arthur," said a loud voice. "The proof is in your hand.

You are the true-born son of a king, and you will be King of the Britons."

Arthur looked round and saw that tall, hooded figure for a third time. The man threw back his hood to reveal a face that was both old and young, his eyes a deep, forest green, his white hair swept off his high, pale forehead.

"Merlin!" said Sir Ector. "I should have known you were behind all this."

Arthur had heard tales of the legendary Merlin, although till that moment he had never suspected the wizard might actually be real.

Arthur, however, was more interested in what Merlin had said than in the wizard's fame.

"But Sir Ector is my father," Arthur said. "And he isn't a king."

"I have always loved you as my son, Arthur," said Sir Ector. "But you are not of my blood. Your real father was the great Uther Pendragon himself…"

Arthur listened in utter amazement as Sir Ector told the story. Uther had known of the warlords' plot against him, and had asked Merlin to save his baby son. So one dark, windswept night, Merlin had spirited Arthur away to Sir Ector's castle. Sir Ector had already agreed to bring up Arthur as his own son, and had never told anyone that Uther Pendragon was Arthur's true father.

"I thank you from the bottom of my heart," Arthur said at last. He was deeply moved at the thought of what Sir Ector had done for him. "And I swear that whatever happens in the future, I will always think of you as my father. And you, Kay, will always be my brother – if that is your wish too."

Kay smiled at him and said it was, and the three of them joined hands.

"I've long kept watch over you, Arthur," said Merlin, "and the time has come for you to take your rightful place. It was I who called the warlords and chieftains together – so you could show yourself to them as their king. We need a leader, someone who can unite us against the Saxons once more."

"But I'm too young," said Arthur, self-doubt and fear suddenly filling his heart. "Men like that will never accept me as their leader…will they?"

Merlin just smiled, and told him to put the sword back in the stone.

The next morning, Merlin summoned all the warlords and the chieftains to the courtyard. The pavilion had been taken down in the night, and the sword in the stone was there for all to see. An excited murmur ran through them as they read the writing. Arthur stood behind the crowd with Sir Ector and Kay.

"Behold the test of kingship!" said Merlin. "Each man shall try his hand."

And one by one, the warlords and chieftains did try, but with no success. No matter how they strained, none could pull the sword from the stone.

Then Merlin called for Arthur, and the youth stepped forward and slowly made his way through the crowd. The warlords and chieftains stared at him and muttered suspiciously. Arthur gripped the hilt, and they gasped as he pulled the sword free of the stone, that tingle shooting up his arm again.

Arthur raised the sword on high – but now the crowd was angry.

"It's a trick!" somebody yelled. "Kill the wizard…and the boy!"

Several warriors drew their swords and advanced. And suddenly Arthur realised he was not afraid. He had been waiting for this moment his whole life. He knew what to do, and that he would also know what to do when it came to fighting the Saxons and saving his people from fear and hunger.

Arthur leapt into action, his blade flashing in the morning sunlight as he parried the warriors' savage blows with unbelievable speed and skill, the clang of steel on steel filling the air. He fought like a man, like the king they needed to lead them. And soon he had those fierce warriors at his mercy…

The tingle now filled him from head to foot. Power flashed from his eyes.

"Kneel to your king, Britons!" roared Merlin, and the crowd obeyed.

The legend of King Arthur had begun.

THE FABULOUS GENIE
THE STORY OF ALADDIN & HIS MAGIC LAMP

LONG AGO IN CHINA, A CHEEKY YOUNG SCAMP called Aladdin lived with his widowed mother. His father had died when Aladdin was just a small boy, leaving them no money. So Aladdin's mother had to work hard, day and night, sewing, cleaning, taking in washing, doing anything to keep a roof over their heads.

Even so, they never, ever had enough money, and there were often days when they went hungry. And it has to be said that Aladdin didn't do much to help – although he was always happy and smiling. His mother loved her cheeky son, but she worried about Aladdin. She worried about him a lot.

"What's to become of you when I'm dead and in my grave?" she would wail. "If only you'd get a job, and find some way of making yourself a living…"

"Stop nagging, Mother," Aladdin would reply. A job was the last thing he wanted, for heaven's sake. "Er…something will turn up, you wait and see."

And, amazingly enough, something did turn up…or rather, somebody.

One day, Aladdin was in the market square of his home town. He'd had a busy morning playing practical jokes on the traders and helping himself to their wares, when suddenly he felt a tap on his shoulder. He turned round, and there before him was a man wearing a silk turban and an expensive-looking cloak. The man's deep, dark eyes stared straight at Aladdin – but he was smiling.

"Aladdin, at last I've found you!" said the man. "I am your Uncle Hasan, long-lost brother of your poor, dead father, may his soul rest in peace…"

"Uncle?" said a surprised Aladdin. "You don't look like the kind of person who might be part of my family…besides, I didn't know I even had any uncles."

"Ah, that's my fault, I suppose," said Hasan. "I, er…left the country long before you were born…before your father met your mother, in fact. I should have written, kept in touch a bit more. But anyway, I'm here now, so why don't you take me home to meet your mother? She's still alive, isn't she?"

"Er…yes, she is," said Aladdin, a little unsure about Hasan. But then he decided the man seemed genuine enough. Besides, Aladdin was excited by the idea that he might be related to someone who was obviously wealthy.

So Aladdin took Hasan to his house, and introduced him to his mother.

"Uncle?" she said, suspiciously. "Your father never mentioned a brother. Oh, Aladdin, how many times have I told you not to speak to strangers?"

"Oh dear, I can see I'm going to have to work a little harder at persuading you both," said Hasan. He got out a purse fat with coins and held it up in front of them. "I know, why don't we talk over dinner? Here, Aladdin, take some money, go back to the market, buy us plenty of lamb and rice…"

Hasan paid for a sumptuous meal, and told them about his life while they ate. He said that he and Aladdin's father had been very close, but Hasan had wanted to travel abroad. He thought Aladdin's father had missed him so much he hadn't spoken his name again for fear of breaking down with grief.

Hasan also said he'd done well abroad and was now a rich merchant, but had always wanted to return to China to be reunited with his brother. He had made some inquiries as soon as he'd arrived – and had almost been overcome with grief himself when he'd discovered that his beloved brother had died.

By the end of the meal, Aladdin's mother was totally convinced, too.

And suddenly life was very, very different for them. The next day, their new-found, wealthy relative bought them more food, and some expensive clothes, and paid a year's rent on the house. Then Hasan announced that he would solve their problems forever by setting Aladdin up as a merchant.

"Allah is mighty!" said Aladdin's mother. "It's the answer to my prayers!"

"We might as well get started immediately," said Hasan. "I'll take you on a trading trip with me, Aladdin, and show you how to make some money."

Hasan bought two camels, and he and Aladdin set off that same morning. Hasan led the way and Aladdin followed him, his mother waving goodbye.

"Listen and learn, Aladdin!" she called out. "And make sure you behave!"

Aladdin rolled his eyes, and waved back without looking round. But he had every intention of doing as his mother said. He was keen to make the most of this opportunity, and was quite nervous – which is why he kept up a stream of cheeky chatter as he and Hasan rode out of the city and into the desert. But Hasan was strangely quiet, which only made Aladdin more anxious.

Eventually they arrived at a lonely place. Hasan dismounted from his camel, and Aladdin did the same. Then Hasan walked around, head down, searching the ground with his eyes while Aladdin waited, confused. After a few moments, Hasan seemed to find what he was looking for, and came over to Aladdin.

"I don't understand, Uncle," said Aladdin. "Why have we stopped here?"

"Be quiet, you impudent young wretch!" Hasan snarled, and gave Aladdin such a hard, vicious clout on the side of the head that the poor boy saw stars.

"Owww! What was that for?" Aladdin yelled, shocked by this change.

"For being so irritating," Hasan hissed. "You've been driving me mad with your idiotic chatter. And it was a warning, too. Actually, I'm delighted to say that I'm not your uncle, you sorry excuse for a human being. But I could definitely be your worst nightmare – if you don't do exactly what I say!"

"Well, who are you then?" said Aladdin, massaging his throbbing ear.

"I am, in fact, a Moorish sorcerer," said Hasan, "and through my dark arts I have discovered the whereabouts of a secret treasure cave. It's here, right beneath our feet." Hasan swept some sand aside, and revealed a square stone slab with a large metal handle in its centre. "I also discovered that only a boy called Aladdin could go into the cave."

"Why does it have to be me?" said Aladdin, puzzled. "Or aren't you a good enough sorcerer to know all the answers?"

"Silence, you vile worm!" Hasan snapped. "That's just the way it happens with magic things. Believe me, I wish it was different. It took a long time to find you, and getting your mother to believe me cost a lot of money. But it will all be worth it in the end… now open that door, and be quick about it!"

Aladdin's mind reeled as he tried to take in what he had been hearing. But despite his confusion – and his painful ear – he was still curious…a treasure cave below his feet? So he grabbed the metal handle and pulled, and the slab swung open, revealing a flight of steps leading down into pitch darkness. A musty, dusty smell wafted out, followed by a couple of squeaking bats.

"Right, down you go," said Hasan, his eyes gleaming.

"Actually, I'd rather not," Aladdin said. The darkness and the smell and the bats had put him off, and he wasn't so curious now. But Hasan whipped out a dagger and held it to his throat.

"Er…all right, I'll do it then," Aladdin said.

"Very wise," said Hasan, smiling at him unpleasantly. "All I want is a certain lamp – you'll know which one I mean the instant you see it…"

Aladdin descended the steps, his heart thudding in his chest. At the bottom he found an old torch, and he lit it with a spark from the tinderbox he always carried. He held the torch aloft…and gasped with wonder.

Before him was a huge cavern, the flickering torchlight barely reaching its far side. The light glinted off the heaps of gold and jewels that covered the floor.

There were diamonds and rubies and emeralds and an ocean of gold coins, more treasure than even the Sultan himself could possess.

And in the middle of the cave was a marble plinth bearing a small lamp.

That must be the one, Aladdin thought. He picked it up, and was surprised to see it was an ordinary old oil lamp, quite tarnished, nothing special at all.

Aladdin shrugged, and started making his way back. He stopped here and there to sift through the heaps of treasure, stuffing his pockets with sapphires and pearls and coins, finding among other things a ring he liked the look of. It bore a huge diamond that glittered beautifully in the torchlight. Aladdin stared into its strange depths for a moment, then slipped it onto his finger.

Eventually Aladdin was standing at the bottom of the steps once more.

"At last!" Hasan said quietly, staring at the lamp. "Right, up you come."

"No, actually I, er…don't think I will," said Aladdin, fearing what Hasan might do once he had the lamp in his possession. "I'm happy where I am."

Hasan tried being nice. Hasan begged, and pleaded, and wheedled, and threatened, but Aladdin wouldn't move, and there was nothing Hasan could do. Suddenly it was all too much for Hasan – the long journey, the cheeky chatter, the frustration – he'd had enough of the whole thing. So Hasan lost his temper.

"Very well, stay there!" he roared, and kicked the stone slab shut.

Hasan turned round and stomped away, then climbed on his camel and rode off – and he didn't stop muttering furiously about China and caves and cheeky boys until he arrived back home in Morocco, several months later.

But Aladdin was stuck in the cave. The stone slab was shut fast, and no matter how he heaved and pushed, Aladdin just couldn't shift it. He shouted himself hoarse, but he soon realised he'd been left to die. His torch went out, and he couldn't get it alight again. He sat in the darkness sobbing, calling for his mother, wringing his hands, accidentally rubbing the diamond ring as he did so.

Suddenly a stream of smoke shot out of the ring, strange, glowing, blue smoke that spun itself into a spiral. It whirled and curled and sparkled and gleamed and gradually seemed to grow more solid, until a tall blue muscular figure stood before Aladdin, his turbaned head bowed low. Then the figure lifted his head, and Aladdin saw a pair of piercing blue eyes staring at him.

"Whoa!" said Aladdin, scrambling backwards. "Who…what are you?"

"I am the genie of the ring," the figure boomed. "What is your desire, Master?"

Aladdin thought this genie might be telling the truth. After all, he had appeared as if by magic. And then Aladdin realised that he might have been given a way of saving himself from slowly starving to death in the dark.

"All right, then…" he said, and crossed his fingers. "Get me out of here."

There was a bright blue flash – and Aladdin found himself outside, safe and sound, the genie spiralling back into the ring. Aladdin was very relieved! He danced round happily, then leapt on his camel and rode home to tell his mother what had happened. But she didn't believe his wild story of an uncle who wasn't an uncle but a sorcerer, of genies and treasure, and thought he'd probably just upset Hasan – and lost his chance of becoming a rich merchant. Then when Aladdin showed her the jewels and coins that he'd stuffed in his pockets, she wailed and said he must have stolen them from someone.

"And what's that you've got there?" she said crossly, pointing at the lamp.

"Oh, only an old lamp," said Aladdin, idly rubbing it. A stream of smoke shot out of its spout – a strange, glowing, red smoke that spun itself into a spiral. It whirled and curled and sparkled and gleamed and gradually seemed to grow more solid, until a tall red muscular figure stood before them, his turbaned head bowed low. But this genie was much bigger than the other.

It raised its huge head, and stared at Aladdin with its piercing red eyes.

"I am the genie of the lamp," the figure boomed. "What is your desire, Master?"

"Wow, another one!" said Aladdin, amazed. "This is getting better all the time! You see, Mother, I was telling the truth!"

"Well, Allah bless my soul!" she said. "You were, too!" And then she fainted.

She came round after a while, and by then, Aladdin had discovered that the genie of the lamp could give them more or less whatever they wanted.

For a while Aladdin just had fun, ordering the genie to bring them even more sumptuous meals than the one Hasan had paid for – the kind of food the Sultan himself might eat, and wonderful clothes, and gorgeous jewels, and perfumes for his mother. Then Aladdin paused, and thought. He would have to be more careful, he realised. A sudden change from poverty to wealth was bound to attract attention, and if anyone found out about his fabulous lamp they might try to steal it. And that would be the end of their good fortune.

Aladdin decided to keep the lamp a secret, and use it sparingly.

So he set himself up as a market trader, and then he became a merchant after all, and within a few years, he was the richest man in the city.

And not long after that, he married the beautiful Yasmin, daughter of the Sultan. They lived in a marvellous palace and were blissfully happy. Aladdin loved Yasmin, and Yasmin loved her husband, and she thought he was a wonderful man, although there was one odd thing about him. He had an old, tarnished, battered lamp that he kept in a cupboard in their bedroom. He seemed to be very attached to it, too, but would never explain why.

At any rate, things were perfect for the young couple – Yasmin even got on with her mother-in-law, who lived with them in their palace – and that's the way they probably would have stayed. If it hadn't been for Hasan.

The Moorish sorcerer had almost forgotten his experiences in China, but then one day, he decided to check up on what Aladdin was doing. He cast a few magic spells, peered into his crystal ball – and was stunned to see that the cheeky young scamp's fortunes seemed to have changed completely.

"He must have taken the lamp for himself!" Hasan hissed furiously.

Within a few weeks Hasan was back in Aladdin's home town. He knew through his dark arts that the lamp was hidden somewhere secret, and he devised a cunning plan to get his hands on it. He disguised himself as an old man, a seller of lamps, and went to Aladdin's palace one morning when Aladdin was out.

"New lamps for old!" Hasan shouted at the gate. "New lamps for old!"

Aladdin's mother didn't hear him, but Yasmin did, and remembered that old lamp in the cupboard.

What a nice surprise for Aladdin it would be to find a new lamp in its place, she thought. So she took it out to Hasan at the gate. He gave her a new lamp, then quickly hurried away with the old one.

He knew all about the genie in it, and the power the genie could give him.

"At long last!" Hasan cried as he rubbed the lamp and the genie appeared, with all the usual magical special effects, of course. "Genie, take me straight back to Morocco," Hasan said. "Oh, and bring Aladdin's palace, too…"

"Your wish is my command, Master," said the genie, and obeyed Hasan's bidding, whirling him and the palace off in a towering cloud of red smoke.

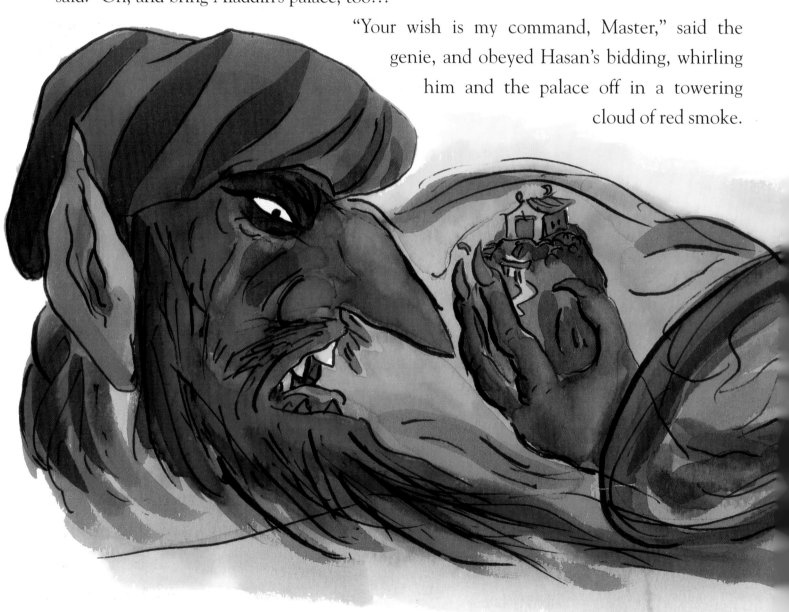

Yasmin was inside it, and so – unluckily for her – was Aladdin's mother.

Aladdin returned later to discover a very nasty surprise – a huge hole where his palace should have been. He was horrified, and worried about his wife and mother, but no one could tell him what had happened. Aladdin had his suspicions, and remembered that he also had a way of finding out for sure. He had kept a certain diamond ring for just this kind of emergency.

He rubbed it, and soon the genie of the ring was standing before him. The genie told Aladdin about Hasan's trick, and how the genie of the lamp had taken the palace – and Yasmin and Aladdin's mother – to Morocco. But the genie of the ring wasn't powerful enough to bring them and the palace back.

"Right, then," Aladdin said grimly. "I'll have to sort this out myself."

So Aladdin got the genie of the ring to take him to Morocco. The genie of the lamp had dumped Aladdin's palace by the sea, and Aladdin crept inside, keeping an eye out for Hasan. But the sorcerer didn't appear, and Aladdin soon found Yasmin and his mother. They were very glad to see him.

"Oh, Aladdin," Yasmin wailed. "You must save me from that horrible old man. He says I have to forget about you and agree to be his wife instead…"

But Aladdin was cleverer than Hasan and he quickly came up with a plan to deal with the sorcerer once and for all. Some say he got

Yasmin to give Hasan a poisoned drink. Others claim that Aladdin hid behind a curtain, then jumped out on the unsuspecting sorcerer and stabbed him. But the truth is funnier.

Aladdin told the genie of the ring to shrink Hasan to the size of a mouse, then seal him in a magic bottle with a tiny replica of Aladdin himself. And that's where Hasan is to this day, trapped inside forever, listening to an endless stream of cheeky chatter and jokes, unable to do anything about it.

Aladdin found his fabulous lamp, and told the genie to whisk them home in the palace. And that's pretty much the end of the story, except to say that Aladdin and Yasmin had many fine children and lived happily ever after.

Oh, and Aladdin's mother lived for a long time too, and never had to work again, so she was very grateful to her son. Although every once in a while, she would look at him and say, "I still think you should have got a proper job."

But then you can never satisfy some people, can you?

It was a lovely spring morning, and Tell enjoyed walking with his son through the Alpine forests and meadows. But when they arrived in Altdorf, Tell soon felt uneasy. There were dozens of Austrian soldiers in the streets, and the Swiss people who were out hurried along, their heads down.

"Why does everyone look so worried, Father?" Walter asked.

"I don't know," said Tell. "But I don't think we'll stay long…"

They went into the market square, where Tell always bought the family's provisions. The stalls were there as usual, but both buyers and sellers were quiet, subdued. Tell and Walter headed for the first stall they wanted, but to get to it they had to pass through an open space in the heart of the square.

A tall pole stood at the centre of the space, and perched on top of it was a man's hat – a big, expensive-looking hat decorated with peacock feathers. A couple of Austrian soldiers were standing by the pole, leaning on their pikes and talking to each other, watching Tell and Walter as they approached.

Tell thought it was odd for there to be a hat on a pole in the middle of the market square…but he just shrugged, and decided to ignore it. He put his arm round Walter's shoulders, and they kept right on walking. Suddenly the soldiers shouted, and came running after them. Tell stopped and turned, making sure that his son was behind him. Walter peeked at the soldiers.

They stood glaring at Tell, their pikes lowered and pointing at him.

"You know the new rule," snarled one of them. "And you'd better obey it pretty sharpish, too, my man, or you'll find yourself in serious trouble."

"New rule?" said Tell, puzzled. "I'm sorry, I've been away for a while."

Tell could see that a large crowd was beginning to gather, more soldiers arriving, the buyers and sellers from the market watching the scene closely.

"Very well, I'll explain it," the soldier said slowly, as if Tell were stupid. "Everyone who passes through the square has to bow to the governor's hat."

"The new governor thinks you Swiss peasants need to be taught a lesson," said the other soldier. "Even his hat is more important than any of you!"

Tell looked up at the hat perched on the pole, then returned his gaze to the soldiers. They grinned at each other, and then at him. Tell frowned. He knew his safest move would be to obey their rule. But he also knew the rule was meant to humiliate the Swiss people, to make them feel they were nothing.

He understood now why everyone in Altdorf looked cowed and beaten. This was the last straw, Tell thought. The Austrians had gone too far.

"So what are you waiting for?" said the first soldier. "Let's see you bow."

"I can't do that," Tell said quietly, his voice steady. "No – I won't do that."

The crowd murmured in surprise, and the grins instantly vanished from the soldiers' faces. They blustered, and shook their pikes at Tell, and tried to make him do what they said. But Tell just stood there in front of them, his arms folded and his face set, staring them down with his steely blue eyes.

And if the truth was known, this impressive, strong-looking man made the Austrian soldiers feel uneasy. The crowd sensed this, and the murmurs grew.

"Right then," said the soldier who had spoken first, raising his pike and glowering at the crowd. "I think we'll see what the governor has to say about all this. It's unlucky for you that he chose today to visit this rotten little town, my stubborn friend. He'll soon sort you out. Don't let him get away, men!"

The soldier marched off into a large tavern on one side of the square. Several other soldiers moved forward to guard Tell, while the rest formed a cordon round the square, facing the crowd, pikes lowered. A few moments later the first soldier emerged from the tavern, followed by another man.

Tell knew immediately it was Gessler. The governor was tall and fleshy, had a mean, arrogant face, and wore rich clothes and lots of golden chains and rings. Gessler kept his cold eyes fixed on Tell as he crossed the square. He stopped in front of Tell,

who noticed Gessler had a napkin in one hand, an apple in the other.

"I hate having my lunch interrupted," Gessler said, scowling. "It does terrible things to my digestion…now, why won't you bow to my hat?"

"I just won't, that's all," said Tell, and scowled back at the Austrian.

"Well, we can't have that, can we?" said Gessler. Then he turned to the soldier who had fetched him. "You know what to do, man," Gessler snapped. "Arrest him, and don't bother me again. He's only a stupid, ignorant Swiss peasant – and I've got far more important things on my plate, ha ha!"

Gessler started walking away towards the tavern, laughing at his own joke and holding his napkin over his nose. Tell tensed, and several of the soldiers moved forward nervously to do as Gessler had ordered, the crowd muttering. But just then Walter jumped out from behind his father.

"My father's not stupid, and he's not a peasant!" he yelled. "He's William Tell, a great hunter and the best shot with a crossbow in all of Switzerland!"

"Is that so?" said Gessler, stopping in his tracks. He came back to stand in front of Tell, looked him up and down. "Are you really such a good shot?"

"Yes, he is!" shouted someone in the crowd. "And you should let him go!"

"Perhaps I will," said Gessler. "If he shows me what he can do…"

Gessler paused and tossed the apple he was holding to Tell. "Could you hit that at a hundred paces?" he said, smiling. "You'll leave here a free man if you can."

"I could," said Tell, and tossed the apple straight back to Gessler.

"You're very confident," murmured Gessler, still smiling. "So maybe we'd better make it a little more difficult for you. We need something to rest the apple on, but what? I know! How about somebody's head?"

Then Gessler's smile vanished, and he stared at Tell. "Your son, for example?" he said.

The crowd gasped again. Tell reached out and pulled Walter to him.

"No, it's far too risky," he said. "I refuse to put my son in danger."

"Ah, but you already have," said Gessler, his voice silky smooth now. He was obviously enjoying himself. "Your choice is simple, Tell. Make the shot – or I'll have your son put to death right here. What do you say?"

The crowd fell silent now, shocked by Gessler's threat. Tell wondered if he and Walter could get away. But there were too many soldiers, and Tell realised it would be impossible.

He raged inside, told himself he'd been a fool to come to Altdorf today, and a bigger fool not to bow to the hat.

But then Walter spoke, his voice suddenly breaking into Tell's thoughts.

"You can do it, Father," said Walter, taking Tell's hand. "I know you can."

Tell looked into his young son's eyes and saw the trust there, the unshakeable belief that his father could make this difficult shot and save their lives. Walter wasn't afraid – and Tell knew he couldn't let him down.

So Tell nodded at Gessler, let go of Walter, and unslung his crossbow.

"Put the boy in front of the tavern door," said Gessler, still smiling, not taking his eyes off Tell for a second. "That's near enough a hundred paces."

A couple of the soldiers took Walter to the tavern door. Gessler followed, and carefully placed the apple on Walter's head. Then Gessler walked back to Tell, the crowd watching them silently from beyond the soldiers' pikes.

"Well, then," said Gessler, standing close to Tell, whispering in his ear. "This is it, your moment of truth. Fire whenever you're ready…peasant."

Gessler stood to the side, smirking. Tell looked at him, then took two bolts from his quiver. He fitted one in the crossbow, and slipped the other into his belt where he could get to it more quickly. He raised the crossbow – and paused.

Tell looked along the bolt and over the cobbles in front of him. The world narrowed to the small figure of Walter in the distance, and the even smaller green dot on his son's head. A blood-filled image of what would happen if he fired too low popped into Tell's mind, and he quickly pushed it out again.

Walter smiled at his father. Tell took a deep breath, held it, aimed. Then he breathed out slowly, squeezing the trigger as he did so. Suddenly the crossbow's string twanged, the sound loud in the hush, and the bolt flew towards Walter, a deadly blur followed by every pair of eyes in the square.

The bolt THWACKED into the tavern door, the apple exploding in a shower of green and white pieces, and Walter raised his arms in triumph.

The crowd exploded too, yelling, cheering, calling out Tell's name. They moved forwards, the soldiers looking even more uneasy and backing off.

Walter ran to his father, and Tell fell to his knees to hug his son.

"Very touching," sneered Gessler, his smirk gone. "And I suppose it was good shooting. But one thing puzzles me, Tell. Why did you take two bolts?"

"The second was for you, Gessler, if anything had gone wrong," said Tell, angry, but deeply relieved. He rose to his feet. "Come on, Walter, let's go…"

"Not so fast, Tell!" snapped Gessler. "You heard him, men! He's just admitted he wanted to assassinate me, the emperor's governor! Arrest him!"

If the crowd had been angry before, Gessler's words simply helped to make them furious. There were catcalls and boos and suddenly things were being thrown at the

Austrians – cabbages and eggs and clods of earth, even cobbles. The soldiers pushed back at the crowd, and Tell saw his chance.

"Run, Walter!" he yelled, "Into the crowd – they'll take care of you!"

Walter didn't need to be told twice. He ducked past the soldiers advancing on his father, and dived through the legs of those facing the crowd. At the same time Tell jumped on to the nearest market stall, quickly fitting the second bolt into his crossbow. He levelled it at the soldiers, who stopped.

"You've just signed your own death warrant, and that of your family," Gessler snarled, his eyes full of hate. "You won't get out of this square alive, and so long as there is breath in my body, it will be my mission to make sure your whole family is tracked down and killed. I'll do it, believe me I will."

"Oh, I believe you, Gessler," said Tell, swinging his crossbow in the governor's direction. "And that's why you leave me with no choice."

Tell pulled the trigger for a second time that morning, and the bolt flew straight into the Austrian governor's evil heart. Gessler slumped to the ground and died instantly.

The crowd fell silent again for a brief moment, and the soldiers stood looking shocked and confused. Then the crowd roared and surged forward like a great beast, sweeping the hated soldiers away.

A few seconds later, the pole – and Gessler's hat – came crashing down.

By the end of that morning there wasn't a single Austrian soldier left in Altdorf. The people had sent them all packing, and revelled in their freedom. Tell had found Walter safe and unharmed, but the people wouldn't let them go home. They carried Tell and his son round on their shoulders, cheering.

Eventually they put Tell on a market stall, and he spoke to them.

"I learned something today," said Tell, his strong voice filling the whole square. "I wanted a safe, happy life for my family, but there's only one way to make sure of that. We've brought freedom to one Swiss town – now we have to bring it to the whole of Switzerland. Down with the Austrians!"

The crowd roared again, and soon messengers were hurrying to villages and towns all over Switzerland. It was the beginning of a war of liberation. As Tell stood in the market square of Altdorf with his arm round Walter, he knew there were difficult times ahead. But there was no going back now.

The Swiss people did eventually free themselves from the Austrians, and William Tell played a leading part in the long struggle. He is remembered to this day as a hero in Switzerland, and all around the world – a simple, honest man who loved his family, and who was finally pushed too far by a tyrant.

And as the man who shot an apple for his country's freedom.

SUPERHERO

THE STORY OF HERCULES & THE MONSTROUS CACUS

HERCULES STRODE DOWN THE TRACK, whistling happily to himself in the late afternoon sunlight. He was a strapping, muscular youth wearing the pelt of a huge lion as a cloak, and carrying an enormous club over his shoulder. And shambling along in front of him was a large herd of beautiful white cattle.

"Whoa, my lovelies!" Hercules said, and started shoving the beasts off the path. "I think we'll stop here for the night. It looks as good a place as any."

To one side of the track was a big field, with some low, rocky hills beyond that. On the other, the land sloped towards a village on the bank of a river. Hercules quickly got the herd settled, then made camp, lighting a fire and cooking himself something to eat as the sun set and the stars came out.

When he had finished eating, Hercules wrapped himself in his cloak and lay down to sleep. It had been a good day, he thought, as he listened to the gentle lowing of the cattle nearby, and the sound of them munching on the juicy grass.

Another of his twelve labours achieved, and only two more to go, thought Hercules.

Life had been very difficult for Hercules recently. He was famous for his incredible strength and courage, and he had performed many heroic deeds. But he had fallen foul of the gods, mostly because they were jealous, and found himself forced to serve as a slave to a certain King Eurystheus. Of course Hercules could never be an ordinary slave. And King Eurystheus was a mean, nasty man who thought the gods wanted him to punish Hercules.

So he told Hercules he could have his freedom back if he completed twelve labours, the only snag being that they seemed utterly impossible.

Hercules took the labours on, though, and achieved them one by one. He slew man-eating beasts and hideous monsters, tamed terrifying mad bulls, caught magic horses who could run faster than the wind, even killed an evil giant with three heads who owned a herd of white cattle. Those were the cattle mooing in the field while Hercules rested beneath the stars. The cattle were famously beautiful beasts and Eurystheus was keen to acquire them.

So Hercules knew that this task – his tenth – wouldn't be complete until he returned to the king's palace with the herd and handed it over to the king. He also knew Eurystheus had been told exactly how many cattle there were…

But something strange happened while Hercules lay dreaming of his future freedom, a smile on his lips. A massive boulder seemed to move by itself in the hills, revealing a hidden cave. A large, dark shape crept out into the field, and slithered up to the cattle. The shape sniffed, and chuckled.

"Ah, fresh meat," the dark shape murmured happily in an evil voice. "I'll have some of these. They'll do nicely for my breakfast in the morning…"

The dark shape was, in fact, a hideous creature called Cacus, a ghastly, foul cross between a giant and a monster with tentacles. Cacus lived in the hidden cave and terrorised the countryside, grabbing any animals and people it encountered and dragging them back to the cave to eat them alive.

It was a dark, moonless night, and Hercules' campfire had gone out by then, so Cacus didn't see the superhero. Cacus seized half a dozen cattle and carried them off, the poor beasts being too surprised to moo in protest.

Soon the boulder was in place again, and Hercules slept on, blissfully unaware.

The sun rose a few hours later, and the warm rays on his face woke him. Hercules stood up, stretched, thought about breakfast, glanced at the herd – and froze. He could tell immediately it was smaller than it should have been – and when he counted the cattle, he discovered six were missing.

"Oh, no!" Hercules muttered unhappily to himself. "That's all I need…"

He wondered if the six cattle had just wandered off and got lost, but he didn't think it was likely. He'd discovered that as a herd they tended to stick together. Hercules decided it was more probable that someone – perhaps a gang of sneaky, rat-faced, good-for-nothing cattle thieves – had stolen them.

Hercules frowned, angry with himself for not staying alert. But he was more angry with whoever had stolen the cattle and put at risk his chance of regaining his freedom. If Eurystheus didn't get the whole herd, Hercules knew he'd just give him more labours to complete. Hercules was determined to get the animals back, and teach the thieves a lesson they'd never forget.

He checked the ground for any tracks that might show him who had taken the cattle, and in which direction they might have gone. There were plenty of hoof prints in the field, but during the night the remaining cattle had walked all over the giant's tracks, so nothing was clear.

He stood in the field for a second, thinking. He glanced up at the low, rocky hills, then turned to look down at the little village in the distance.

"Umm…maybe somebody there can help me," Hercules murmured.

He made sure the rest of the cattle were all right, then set off at a trot, carrying his enormous club. A few minutes later he entered the village.

It was a scruffy, smelly, run-down place with a muddy track for a high street, where a few chickens pecked in the dirt. The houses were little more than mud huts huddling up against each other as if they were scared of something, and nobody seemed to be about. Hercules came to a halt.

"Hello?" he called out, his voice echoing. "Is anybody here?"

There was no answer, although the chickens did squawk and scurry away.

Hercules was puzzled. He strode over to a hut and knocked on the door. It opened a crack, and the pale face of a frightened man looked out at him.

"Y-y-yes?" the man said, nervously. "What do you want?"

"I'm looking for some of my cattle," said Hercules. "I think they've probably been stolen, and I want them back. Do you happen to know…"

"Aaaaargh!" screamed the man. "It must have been Cacus!"

And with that, the man slammed his door in Hercules' face. Hercules was more puzzled now. He wondered who this Cacus might be, so he went to the next hut and knocked on the door. But the same thing happened there, and at the next hut where Hercules knocked, and the next, and the next.

Hercules finally lost his patience. He marched back to the first hut, kicked in the door as if it were made of paper, and dragged out the man from inside.

"Right," said Hercules, grim-faced. He gripped the squirming man by his tunic and held him up in the air at arm's length. "I want some answers."

Suddenly the man became very, very talkative. He explained about Cacus being the local fire-breathing half-giant half-monster, said he thought it had certainly been Cacus who'd taken the cattle, and finished by asking Hercules – in a polite voice – if there was anything else he would like to know.

"Yes, there is," said Hercules. "Where can I find this…Cacus?"

"In the hills on the other side of the t-t track," the man stammered, "although nobody knows exactly where. We think he's got a hidden cave."

"Thanks," said Hercules, releasing his grip and dropping him.

Hercules turned on his heel and strode out of the village. Most of the other villagers opened their doors to peek at him, but Hercules took no notice. He was already scanning the hills to see if he could tell where Cacus had his den.

It didn't take him long to find it. There was something on the flank of the hill that looked like the entrance to a big cave, although it was blocked by a boulder. There were some strange, slithery tracks there too – they seemed to go up to the boulder, then disappear underneath it. Hercules climbed to the top of the hill. He put an ear to the ground and listened, then smiled, and dug his hands deep into the soil till he reached the rock that formed the hill itself.

Then he took hold, and using all his strength, he pulled. There was a tremendous sound of wrenching and tearing…and the top of the hill came off. Hercules tossed it behind him, where it landed with a terrific CRASH! on another of the hills, and he peered down into the large hollow space below.

Looking up at him was a surprised Cacus. The giant had one of the white cattle gripped in his tentacles, and was on the point of biting into it.

"Ugh, what a disgusting smell," said Hercules, waving his hand in front of his face. It was true – an absolutely vile stench was wafting out of the cave now it was open to the air. Cacus was squatting on a heap of bones and other unspeakable remains, and Hercules, who had seen plenty of monsters in his time, thought this was definitely the foulest creature he'd ever encountered.

But at least the cattle were still alive, Hercules thought. He had noticed the other five beyond Cacus, squeezed up together against the cave wall.

"Hey, how dare you do that to my cave!" Cacus growled. "How would you like it if someone ripped the top off your house? Who are you, anyway?"

"My name is Hercules," our hero replied. "More importantly, I'm the man you stole those cattle from last night…but if you give them back to me without any argument we'll say no more about it, and I'll be on my way."

Cacus put down the cow, and an evil grin spread over his face.

"You must be joking," said the giant. He started to climb the cave wall. "They'll make a tasty breakfast. And I think I'll have you for my lunch…"

Hercules backed off a little, and watched Cacus emerge. Cacus really was an unpleasant sight, Hercules thought. The awful creature had a man's body, a huge one, but where there should have been arms and legs there were clusters of writhing tentacles. He had a leering face, too, and a mouth full of huge fangs.

"Look, I don't want any trouble," said Hercules. "I just want what's mine."

"You don't want any trouble?" hissed Cacus, slithering wetly to a stop. "Well, I'm afraid that's what you're going to get. Observe, and tremble!"

Cacus reared up and roared, the creature's vile breath making Hercules turn his face and cover his nose. Then Cacus started spitting big fireballs, and Hercules had to dodge out of their way. Soon the grass and bushes and trees on the hillside were burning, and thick smoke swirled around them.

"Ha, what do you think of that?" roared Cacus. "Not that it matters. For now comes the part where I grab you with my tentacles and tear you to pieces…"

Cacus slithered forward again, smacking his lips, his tentacles writhing.

Hercules gave a deep sigh, and hefted his club in his hand. He waited till the tentacles were almost upon him…then he leapt over them, bringing his club crashing down on the creature's head. There was a loud CRACK! and Cacus fell to the ground, stunned, his eyes rolling upwards in his skull. Then Hercules grabbed a bunch of tentacles in his free hand, lifted Cacus up, and started swinging him round in the air. Cacus whizzed round once, twice…

And on the third circuit, Hercules let him go. Cacus flew off into the sky faster than a speeding arrow, his tentacles trailing behind him like the tail of a comet. Soon he was a tiny dot, and then he vanished. Hercules knew he'd come down miles away in the sea, and that would be the end of him. Hercules rubbed his sticky hands on his lionskin cloak and turned away.

"Another job well done," he said. "Shame it's not on the list, though."

Hercules went back up the hill and – holding his nose – jumped into the cave. He shoved the boulder out of the entrance, and led the six stolen cattle back to the rest of the herd in the field. He got them all on to the track and moving in the right direction – then suddenly a crowd of people appeared.

"Wait! Don't go!" one of them shouted. It was the man who had told Hercules about Cacus. The rest of the villagers jostled behind him, all of them looking much happier now. "We saw what you did," said the man. "You're amazing! Who are you? Please, stay here and be our king!"

"Sorry," said Hercules. "I'm afraid I can't…there are some things I have to do." The villagers looked disappointed at his words. "You'll be all right from now on, though," Hercules said. "I mean, without Cacus around you might be able to make a bit more of your village. Er…what's it called, anyway?"

"Rome," said the villagers, smiling at him. Hercules smiled back.

"Oh, yes," he said, urging the beautiful white cattle on down the track. "Er…I can just see it – one day you'll have a big, beautiful city here, spread out over these hills and along the river. All the best, then…bye!"

Hercules strode off into the distance, whistling cheerfully once more.

He did complete his twelve labours. He regained his freedom at last from Eurystheus, and went on to perform many more legendary deeds. As Hercules had predicted, Rome did become a beautiful city, and a very powerful one, too. And the people of Rome never forgot the hero who had given them their freedom from fear, holding a great festival every year in his honour.

THE FANTASTIC VOYAGE OF SINBAD

THE STORY OF SINBAD THE SAILOR & THE ROC

T HERE ONCE LIVED IN THE CITY OF BAGHDAD a young man called Sinbad, whose father was a rich merchant. Sinbad's father died when Sinbad was still a boy, leaving his son plenty of money. But as soon as he was old enough, Sinbad took to wild living, and it wasn't long before he had spent his entire fortune.

One morning Sinbad woke up – his head throbbing after yet another party – and realised he was in trouble. He had no money, and unless he found a way of making some more, he knew he'd probably end up as a beggar on the streets. The answer, he decided, was to become a merchant like his father.

So Sinbad sold his house and furniture, and scraped enough money together to buy some merchandise. Then he said goodbye to his friends, and set sail on a trading ship with a number of other merchants. And to begin with, as the ship sailed from port to port and the merchants traded, things went well. Sinbad soon realised he was sure of making a decent profit on the voyage, and he began to feel happy and confident about his future again.

Then one day, as the ship was heading for home, the lookout man caught sight of a small island. The ship needed fresh water, and besides, the sailors and the merchants wanted to stretch their legs on dry land. The captain dropped anchor, and the crew and passengers went ashore, Sinbad among them.

It was a very beautiful place, with fields of exotic flowers, a forest of fruit trees, and a sparkling stream running down from the hills. The sailors and merchants soon spread out over the beach, but Sinbad strolled away from his companions and headed inland. Eventually he came to a tall tree on the edge of a clearing. He sat down beneath it, and being rather tired, he fell asleep.

Sinbad woke a few hours later, feeling refreshed and relaxed, and made his way back to the beach, expecting to meet his companions there. But the beach was completely empty – and when Sinbad looked for the ship, all he could see was a small dot slipping over the horizon. They had sailed without him! He could only think that no one had noticed he had been missing…

Whatever the reason, Sinbad was marooned on the island, and everything he possessed in this world – his merchandise and his money, his salvation and the beginning of his new fortune – was simply vanishing before his eyes. Sinbad waited, hoping someone on board the ship would discover the mistake and make the captain return for him… But with every minute that went by, Sinbad knew that such a rescue became less and less likely.

After a while, he sank to his knees and wept bitter tears.

If he'd thought he was in trouble before, he knew that he was in an even bigger mess now. He wished that he had never left Baghdad. He cursed his evil luck, and wondered if he was doomed to end his days alone, far from his homeland and friends. Then he slowly started to pull himself together.

"This won't do," he muttered, drying his eyes. "God helps those who help themselves, they say. And maybe things aren't really as bad as I think they are."

Sinbad decided it would probably be a good idea to know more about the island. So he returned to the tall tree and climbed right to the top.

There were no signs of people or settlements, the island's interior being almost filled with trees – but there was something in the distance, something strange…

Sinbad couldn't be sure, but it looked like a large, perfectly white hill.

He climbed down from the tree and set off to investigate. It took him quite some time to reach what he'd seen, and the thick forest prevented any more glimpses of it until he arrived at the spot. Sinbad pushed back the last, low-hanging branch…and stood transfixed by the amazing sight before him.

It was an enormous dome. Much bigger than the biggest mosque in Baghdad – its surface smooth and hard as stone to the touch. Sinbad slowly walked round it, but he could discover no entrances or windows anywhere, nor any clue to what this object might be, nor whether it had a purpose.

Then suddenly, a dark shadow fell over the dome, and Sinbad too.

He looked up at the sky, and saw something even more amazing. A bird was descending from the clouds – but this bird was of colossal size, almost bigger than the city of Baghdad itself, thought Sinbad, let alone its biggest mosque. He realised the bird was heading straight for the white dome, and he panicked.

Sinbad dived for the cover of the forest undergrowth as the bird landed on the dome. Then he turned to look. The bird brought its enormous wings into its sides and stuck its legs out behind, flattening several trees in the process.

It squawked with a noise like thunder, went quiet, and settled comfortably.

"Just like a hen brooding on an egg…" Sinbad murmured in his hiding place. Suddenly he remembered a story one of the sailors on the ship had told him about a legendary bird of enormous size – a creature called a Roc. Sinbad realised it wasn't legendary after all, it was real, and that the white dome must be the great beast's egg, with a giant baby Roc inside it. Sinbad stood there thinking for a moment, and a daring plan began to form in his mind. The Roc obviously didn't spend all her time sitting on the egg – Sinbad had just seen her returning from a flight to somewhere else. What if he hitched a ride with her the next time she flew away? He had nothing to lose. He was sure that wherever it went had to be better than this island.

The sun was setting, and darkness was creeping through the trees. This was as good a time as any, thought Sinbad – the Roc probably wouldn't fly off during the night. Sinbad tiptoed out of the undergrowth and made for one of the Roc's enormous legs. Then he quickly unwound his turban, and using the material as a rope, he strapped himself to a giant, curved talon.

Now all he had to do was wait – although that was easier said than done.

He barely slept a wink, of course. His whole being was filled with worry about whether his plan would work or not. What if the Roc discovered him in the morning, and pecked at him with her terrible, giant beak? What if the turban material wasn't strong enough to hold him, and he fell from the sky?

It seemed to Sinbad that he had just dozed off when he was suddenly jerked awake. The sun had risen, and as he looked down he saw the ground receding rapidly, the giant white egg growing smaller and smaller, and he realised that the Roc must have taken wing. He held on to the talon as tightly as he could, and prayed that the material of his turban wouldn't tear…

Mercifully it didn't, and after a while Sinbad even began to enjoy his flight through the air. The Roc's great wings beat above his head, the wind blew into his face, and far, far below him was the sea glittering in the morning sunshine, its surface dotted with islands. Eventually the bird crossed a coastline into a landscape of mountains, and began to descend.

The Roc landed at last, jarring every bone in Sinbad's body – but he was alive. He quickly untied his turban before the Roc realised he was there, then rolled away across the ground and towards a large boulder nearby. He hid behind it, amazed he had survived such an incredible journey, and – keen to see where he was, and what the Roc was doing – he took a careful peek out from behind the boulder.

Immediately Sinbad's heart sank.

He saw that he was on a steep, rocky hillside with a deep valley below it, the ground brown and barren and littered with boulders and lots of odd-looking, shiny pebbles. The valley was surrounded by mountains too, huge, forbidding peaks that looked impossible to climb. It was the kind of place you could easily be trapped in forever.

The Roc herself was further down the hillside, pecking at something on the ground. Then she raised her head, and Sinbad saw that she had a giant snake in her beak – and he realised the Roc came here to feed. Sinbad noticed other giant snakes, all of them slithering away from the great bird as fast as they could go. But the Roc rose in the air with her wriggling prey and flew off.

"Oh no, I don't believe it…" Sinbad groaned. He was in an even bigger mess than ever now. "Talk about jumping out of the frying pan and straight into the fire!" he muttered to himself.

"I should have stayed on the island."

At least there he would have had water to drink and fruit to eat, Sinbad thought, and the chance that a ship might come. But there was nothing in this godforsaken valley, nothing except the prospect of death – a lingering death from hunger and thirst, or perhaps a fast but very unpleasant end in the belly of a giant snake. Although they all seemed to have vanished now, he noticed.

Sinbad slumped to the ground, and sat with his back to the boulder feeling very sorry for himself. Soon the sun dipped behind the rim of mountains, and a thick gloom began to steal up from the valley bottom towards him. A sharp wind whipped round the boulder and cut right through his thin clothes.

Sinbad rose and stumbled off, looking for somewhere to shelter for the night. He saw the entrance to a small cave and hurried inside, then sat down. Suddenly he heard a quiet hissing, and he turned round as the last rays of the setting sun came through the entrance to the cave and lit its furthest reaches.

At the back, curled round her eggs, was one of the giant snakes.

Sinbad was so frightened that his hair actually stood on end. The giant snake seemed to be sleeping, but Sinbad was terrified that any movement might wake her. So as the sun disappeared and the cave fell into darkness, Sinbad stayed where he was. He sat there rigid with fear the whole night.

It was too much for him. The second the sun rose in the morning and he saw light at the cave mouth, he scrambled to his feet and ran out, trusting that speed would save him. But he had only taken a few steps when a large object whistled past just above his head, and landed with a SPLAT! in front of him.

It rolled down the slope a little way, and Sinbad followed it, curious. But when he saw what it was, he recoiled in disgust, for it was the rotting carcass of a very dead sheep. Then he glanced at it again, and realised that a number of those odd-looking, shiny pebbles had become stuck in the slimy flesh…

And that's when he remembered another story he'd heard on the ship.

A sailor had spoken of the legendary Diamond Mountains, a place where a great valley floor was carpeted with diamonds and gems. But they were impossible to get to, so diamond hunters had perfected a cunning scheme.

Each morning, the sailor had said, the hunters catapulted dead sheep into the valley, knowing that any diamonds the corpses fell on would stick in the flesh. They also knew that during the day giant Rocs would swoop on the carcasses and carry them off to eat. The hunters simply waited on the peaks of the mountains for the birds to pass by on their way out of the valley, then shot arrows and threw stones to frighten them into dropping their carrion. Then all the hunters had to do was pick the diamonds out of the meat.

Sinbad's heart rose. Another plan began to form in his mind. The stones on the ground around him were definitely diamonds, he thought, and he stuffed as many as he could into his pockets. He looked up, and already there was a vast, winged shape circling in the sky. He pulled off his turban once more, tied himself to the carcass with it, and rolled it over so he was underneath.

Then he lay there, his face pressed into the foul corpse, and waited.

A moment or two later he felt a familiar jerking sensation, and knew that the bird had taken the bait. The Roc soared high through the air. Sinbad turned his head slightly and glimpsed the mountain peaks below him. Then suddenly he heard noises, shouting, saw arrows and stones whizzing past.

And then he heard a very loud squawk, and felt the Roc release its burden.

It was only then that Sinbad realised he had no idea how far he had to fall, and he closed his eyes, wondering if he was about to be smashed to a pulp. But, luckily, as he and the dead sheep dropped through the air, the weight of the corpse made it swing right round beneath him. So when they did hit the ground – with an even louder SPLAT! – the carcass cushioned the impact.

Sinbad hurriedly untied his turban and jumped off the rotting meat. He was covered in blood and slime, but he knew as soon as he looked around him that he was on the far side of the mountains, and free of the dreadful valley. Below him was a track that seemed to lead to softer, safer lands.

"In the name of Allah, who – or what – are you?" said a voice behind him.

Sinbad turned round, and saw that he was being watched at a distance by a band of wild-looking men, some carrying bows, some with swords or spears. He realised these must be the diamond hunters, and he stepped forward. The men instantly leapt back, obviously scared of him, and raised their weapons.

"Peace be with you," said Sinbad, holding up his hands, palms outward, to show he meant them no harm. "I am a traveller, and a man just like you."

"But…how did you come to be tied to our bait like that?" said a hunter.

"Ah, that's a long story," said Sinbad, "and one I'm not even sure I believe myself. Still, I'll tell it to you – if you'll help me return to my homeland."

The diamond hunters did help Sinbad, and a few months later his friends were astonished to see him arrive in Baghdad, especially as he had long been given up for dead. They were even more amazed to hear of his adventures, and delighted for him when he sold the diamonds he had collected in the dreadful valley, restoring his entire fortune – and more – at a stroke.

Sinbad bought his old house back and settled down for a while to enjoy a life of luxury. But if his friends thought he would return to his days of wild living, they were wrong. For Sinbad soon grew bored, and forgot the fear and discomfort of his voyage, remembering only the amazing things he had seen and the excitement he had felt. So he decided to go travelling again.

Some people never learn, do they?

THE FEARSOME DRAGON FROM THE LAKE
THE STORY OF GEORGE & THE DRAGON

ONCE THERE WAS A BRAVE KNIGHT CALLED GEORGE who had vowed to fight evil wherever he found it. He had been born in poverty and grown up an orphan, then became a soldier and learnt the acts of war. But he saw that the world was full of evil, and one day he decided to do his best to fight it. After many battles, he heard that an evil dragon was terrifying the city of Silena in Libya, and headed there to see what he could do to help its people.

George came riding out of the desert on a beautiful white horse, the morning sun rising behind him and casting a fiery orange glow over the sand. His armour shone, he carried a lance under his right arm, and he held the horse's reins in his left hand. His sword was in its sheath on his left hip, and his shield was strapped to his back.

He knew Silena wasn't far now. Soon he rode up a steep slope to the crest of a ridge, and stopped there to look down. Below him and to his left was the city, surrounded by its high stone walls. To his right was a large lake, the water dark and strangely still.

And between the city and the lake stretched a broad, level plain, with a post on a small mound right in the middle of it.

"Umm, that seems odd," George murmured to himself, spurring his horse on. They descended, the downward track taking them past the lake. Now that he was closer to it, George could see it wasn't quite as still as he'd thought.

It seemed to be hot, with grey wisps of steam drifting over it, and from time to time bubbles broke the oily surface with a thick plopping sound.

George trotted on, towards the post. The ground around it was blackened and burned, and, here and there, George saw what seemed to be charred bones. He frowned, gripped his lance more tightly, and urged his horse into a gallop, making for the gates of the city ahead of him. There was no time to lose, he thought. Things were obviously as bad as he'd heard.

George reined his horse in before the gates, which were tall and wooden and reinforced with iron bars and studs. But they were also blackened and scorched, as were the city walls on either side.

George dismounted from his horse, and was just about to knock on one of the gates with a mail-clad fist, when both started to creak open. George quickly moved back, and waited.

A strange procession emerged. First there came some soldiers armed with spears and bows, and behind them was an old horse-drawn cart. Standing in it was a girl, her face pale and frightened and her hands tied. And behind the cart walked a man with the saddest expression that George had ever seen.

The soldiers stopped when they noticed George, and looked confused.

"Who are you, stranger?" said the sad-faced man. "Why have you come to this accursed place? Did you not know that great evil plagues my kingdom?"

"I do know it," said George, realising the man must be the King of Silena. "And that is why I have come. I will gladly fight this evil for you, my lord."

"What, you want to fight the dragon of the lake?" spluttered one of the soldiers.

"You wouldn't be saying that if you'd seen the creature, oh no!"

"He's right," said another soldier. "It's enormous, it breathes fire, it's got teeth like giant razors, and huge claws that can rip a person to red tatters…"

"Besides," added yet another soldier. "There's no need to fight the dragon. All we have to do is keep it fed for a while, and then it will leave us alone."

"Keep it fed?" George murmured. "What does such a monster eat?"

The soldiers looked at each other uneasily, and glanced up at the girl standing in the cart. She had stayed silent so far. But now she spoke.

"People," she said, quietly. "Or rather, one human being a day. That's what it said it wanted, or it would burn the whole city down – and kill us all."

"So every evening we draw lots to see who will be the morning's victim," said the king, his voice cracking. "Today it is Sabra, my own daughter…"

"And I am happy to give my life for our people, Father," she said, although George could tell that she wasn't happy about it, and neither was her father.

"Yes, well, it's only fair," said the first soldier who had spoken, the others muttering in agreement. "We should all take the same risk in the lottery."

"And what if the lottery never ends?" said George. "What if the dragon doesn't leave you alone, and keeps coming back every day for more?" The soldiers didn't reply, although George could see that he had spoken their thoughts for them, the worries they would not admit to. "It will kill you all eventually," he said. "No, this kind of evil must be fought and conquered."

"But what makes you think you can fight the dragon?" jeered another soldier. "You're only a man, and your weapons won't be any use against it."

"I have more than just my lance and sword and shield," George replied. "I have faith…I believe I can do it. And every evil surely has its weak spot…"

Suddenly there was a noise from the lake, and they all looked round. An extra-large bubble had burst on the surface with a loud PLOP! and several more bubbles followed it. Soon the surface was bubbling steadily, as if something was stirring in the depths below and heating up the water.

"Well, you do what you like," muttered one of the soldiers in a panicky voice. "But I'm for sticking with things as they are. Let's get her ready!"

The soldiers quickly led the cart to the mound, pulled the Princess Sabra out, and tied her to the post, continually glancing over their shoulders at the lake as they did so. Then they ran back to the city gates as fast as they could go, dragging the king with them, not even giving him time to say goodbye.

They scrambled inside, and quickly pushed the gates shut behind them.

George walked to his horse, which had been waiting patiently, and re-mounted. He slipped his shield onto his left arm, hefted his lance in his right, and trotted to the mound, reining in his horse and stopping to one side of it.

The princess turned to look at him, her face even paler than before.

"There's still time for you to save yourself, you know…" she said.

"I'm here to save you, Princess," said George, keeping his eyes on the lake. The bubbling was growing stronger and stronger, the plopping louder. The sun was high in the sky, and George was sweating beneath his armour.

He could hear noise behind him, and looked round to see the soldiers and the king and a large crowd of people lining the top of the city walls to watch.

"But you won't be able to save me," wailed the princess. And then she gasped. For a huge shape had broken the surface of the lake, a scaly head with enormous red eyes and a great, grinning mouth full of glittering teeth. Water cascaded from it as the dragon rose further, its vast body and legs appearing. It slowly crawled out and stood dripping. Its green body shiny and wet, so big it almost blotted out the sun. A vision of pure evil, thought George…

The beast stared hungrily, first at him, and then at the princess.

"Well, well, what's this?" said the dragon, its voice like the sound of a furnace roaring. "A double portion to eat! The king is generous today."

"You won't be eating anyone," said George. "Not now, or ever again."

"Oh, yes?" asked the dragon. Its red eyes gleamed at him, and it smiled, showing even more of its wicked teeth. "And who will stop me? You?"

"Yes, I will!" said George. He slammed shut the visor on his helmet and spurred his horse forward – into a trot, then a canter, then a gallop. He lowered his lance, pointed it at the dragon and charged across the plain, his horse's hooves thundering beneath him and stirring up a cloud of dust.

The dragon was taken by surprise, and George was upon it before the beast could move. The point of the lance struck one of the dragon's forelegs, but the scales were too hard for it to penetrate, and the lance snapped like an old piece of kindling. George could hear the crowd on the city walls groan. He wheeled away, stopped, threw down the piece of lance he still held. Then he drew his sword from the sheath, and it flashed in the sunlight.

"You are beginning to annoy me, human," rumbled the creature. "Let me show you how I usually deal with irritating little gnats who get in my way."

The dragon raised its head, opened its mouth wide – and blasted a huge jet of fire at George. He threw his shield over his head just in time, deflecting the flames to either side of him and his horse. But he could feel that the poor animal beneath him was terrified, and his shield grew hotter and hotter.

The firestorm ended at last, but it left George's shield useless. He tossed it to the side and dismounted, shooing his horse away. Then he stood on the scorched earth, sword in hand, the dragon looming over him. He scanned the creature's colossal body, searching for the weak spot he felt must be there.

But the dragon was covered in overlapping scales, from the top of its head to the tip of its long tail, each of them looking harder than steel. The beast might as well be wearing a giant suit of armour itself, thought George, his heart sinking. But he still believed he could do it, he refused to give up…

"So, it seems that I must try a little harder," growled the dragon. Then it snapped at him, the great jaws suddenly swooping down. George dodged them, then saw from the corner of his eye that a huge leg was heading towards him, its claws extended. He dodged that, too – but then he fell.

He rolled onto his back as the dragon stood over him triumphantly.

"And now I will crush you," roared the dragon, rearing back on its hind legs, preparing to bring its front legs down on the young knight. George lay there underneath the great monster, looking up, wondering what he could do to save himself.

Then suddenly he noticed a spot on the beast's belly that didn't seem to be covered by scales, a soft and unprotected patch of skin.

That was it, thought George, the weak spot!

George scrambled to his feet, ran forward, and plunged his sword into the dragon's belly as far as it would go. There was a moment of utter stillness…

Then the dragon screamed in pain and reared back even further. George pulled his sword free, and fiery hot dragon blood gushed out of the gaping wound, over his blade and his hand. George moved away, and the dragon teetered for a moment…then crashed onto its side, howling and thrashing.

The thrashing and howling stopped after a moment or two. The dragon twitched and finally lay still, a plume of smoke curling from its mouth.

A great cheer rose from the city walls, but George took no notice. He wiped his hand clean of the dragon's blood, sheathed his sword, and walked over to the mound to release the princess from her bonds. She was weeping with relief and gratitude, and soon George was surrounded by a great crowd of people. They lifted him onto their shoulders and carried him into the city.

A feast was held in his honour, and by the end of it, the king had given George a huge reward, and said he wanted George to marry the Princess Sabra and be king after him. But George just smiled, and when he had eaten and drunk a little, he quietly asked if somebody could bring him his horse.

"I thank you for the reward," said George as he climbed into the saddle. "But I have no need of money, so I ask you to give it to the poor of the city. And I thank you for your other offer, too, but I cannot marry – not while there is still evil in the world to be fought and conquered. Farewell!"

With that, George rode out through the city gates and towards the setting sun, a dazzling, upright figure who soon vanished into the fiery glare. He went on to fight more battles, and help people wherever he travelled, and he did so many good deeds that when he died he was made into a holy saint.

A saint who was truly a knight in shining armour.

OPEN SESAME!

THE STORY OF ALI BABA & THE FORTY THIEVES

IT'S A STRANGE FACT, BUT SOMETIMES BROTHERS can be so different from each other in character, you might think they couldn't possibly be from the same family at all. Such was the case with two Persian brothers called Kassim and Ali Baba – and because of it, a curious chain of events was set in motion that cost one of the brothers his life, and changed the other's life – forever.

To put things in a nutshell, Kassim was as greedy, deceitful and arrogant as Ali Baba was generous, honest and good-hearted. Kassim married the daughter of a rich man to get at her father's money when he died; Ali Baba married a girl from a poor family for the simple reason that he loved her. So the two brothers seemed destined to follow very different paths.

Kassim did indeed grow richer and richer, but he always wanted more. Ali Baba, meanwhile, barely made a living as a woodcutter, collecting firewood in the forest to sell in town, but at least he was happy with what he had. He was even happier when he and his wife had a baby son, although things were already tough for them, and it's harder to feed three mouths rather than two.

Still, the years went by, and Ali Baba and his family survived and stayed happy, and their baby son – who was called Ahmed – grew into a fine young man. Then one day, Ali Baba set out as usual for the forest with his donkey, and decided to try his luck in a thicket he rarely visited. He started work, cutting branches and rolling them into a big bundle to load on the donkey, when suddenly he heard galloping horses, and they were coming his way.

Ali Baba could hear the unmistakeable chink of weapons as well, and that made him nervous. So he pushed his donkey into the undergrowth, and scrambled up the nearest tree as quickly as he could. He reached the top and looked down just as a column of horsemen appeared on the forest path. They rode past, and stopped at a wall of rock that stood beyond the thicket.

One glance at their wild, brutal faces told Ali Baba they were bandits.

Ali Baba sat in the tree, trembling with fear, trying to stay concealed and hoping the bandits wouldn't notice the leaves shaking. But then something happened that made Ali Baba stop trembling and his mouth fall open with wonder. One of the bandits – a very cruel-looking man who was obviously their captain, thought Ali Baba – dismounted and stood by the wall of rock.

"OPEN SESAME!" the captain said in a loud, strong voice.

And suddenly a hidden door opened in the rock, revealing a secret cave. The captain strode in, and his men dismounted and followed him. Ali Baba counted them. There were forty bandits – including the captain – and each man was carrying a bulging saddlebag. Ali Baba heard the captain say, "CLOSE SESAME!" from inside the cave, and the hidden door instantly swung shut.

Well, you could – as they say – have knocked old Ali Baba down with a feather. He sat in the tree, amazed by what he'd seen and surprised that the name of a common seed could be magical. He listened to the bandits' horses quietly cropping the grass, and wondered what on earth was going to happen next. Then the door opened again. The forty bandits emerged – their saddlebags empty – and climbed on their horses. The captain said, "CLOSE SESAME!" and the door swung shut, and the robber band galloped away.

Ali Baba waited a good long while before he climbed down from the tree, to be sure that the bandits had actually gone. But he did at last, creeping up to the wall of rock to examine it – and there was no sign of a door at all. Ali Baba stood there scratching his head, deeply curious about what might be inside. Then he wondered if the captain's words might work for him too…

"Open sesame," he whispered, far too nervous to say it as loudly as the captain of the bandits. But the door opened in just the same way as before.

Ali Baba cautiously stepped over the threshold of the cave. The bandits had left a torch burning in a wall sconce, and in its flickering light Ali Baba saw that the cave was much, much bigger than he'd thought – and that its floor was entirely covered in treasure! There were gold and silver cups and plates, shiny gems of all kinds, bags and chests overflowing with coins…in short, there was more wealth in that cave than a poor man like Ali Baba could ever have imagined in his wildest daydreams. He thought the bandits must have been storing their ill-gotten gains in there for years, that perhaps it was even a place where generations of thieves had hidden their booty. Then Ali Baba suddenly realised something else – this was a golden opportunity! The kind of opportunity that didn't happen often in a poor man's life…

Ali Baba grabbed a couple of big bags of gold – the bandits wouldn't miss them from such a vast store, he thought – and hurried out of the cave, remembering to say, "CLOSE SESAME!" as he emerged. The hidden door swung shut, leaving the wall smooth. Then he loaded the bags of gold onto his donkey – alongside the bundle of firewood – and headed for home.

Ali Baba's wife, Ayesha, couldn't believe her eyes when he opened one of the bags and poured out a stream of golden coins in front of her. Now it was her turn to sit with eyes wide and mouth open as Ali Baba explained where the bags of gold had come from. But soon she was so happy at their stroke of good fortune that she danced around the room, then hugged her husband.

"How much have we actually got?" Ayesha said at last, her eyes shining.

"I'm not really sure," said Ali Baba, "and we don't have time to count it. I want to hide it as quickly as possible. If somebody should see that we've got all this gold they might start asking questions, and that's the last thing we need…I think we should keep it a secret – just to be on the safe side."

Ali Baba got Ayesha to help him hide the gold, then went out to sell his firewood as usual. Ayesha, however, couldn't rest until she knew the exact amount of their new-found wealth…and then she had an idea. She wouldn't have time to get the gold out of its hiding place, count it and hide it again before Ali Baba came home. But she would have plenty of time to weigh it.

Being a poor family, they had never had enough money to spend on luxuries such as a set of kitchen scales. Ayesha knew her sister-in-law had some, though. So Ayesha dashed off to Kassim's house to borrow them.

"Kitchen scales?" said Kassim's wife Fatimah, who was as greedy and arrogant as her husband, and had a suspicious mind as well. "Of course I'll lend them to you, my dear. So long as you tell me why you need them."

"Oh, er…no special reason," spluttered Ayesha, who was too honest to feel comfortable telling lies. "I just have to weigh something, that's all."

"Is that so?" said Fatimah, smiling at Ayesha while her mind worked overtime. "Well, you wait here while I fetch them. I won't be a minute."

Fatimah went off to the kitchen and got out her scales. She quickly rubbed a little fat on the bottom of one of the pans, hoping that something of what Ayesha put in the pan might stick to it. Then Fatimah rejoined Ayesha, handed over the scales, and said she needed them back as soon as possible.

Ayesha went home, quickly got out the gold, weighed it and hid it again. Then she returned the scales to her sister-in-law, too happy and excited to notice that one small gold coin had stuck to the fat in the pan. Eagle-eyed Fatimah soon found it, however, and took it straight to her husband.

That evening, Kassim went to see his brother. As soon as Ali Baba opened the door, his heart sank, for Kassim rarely deigned to visit his poor relations.

"So, it seems you've come into some money, Brother," said Kassim, a scowl on his face. "Such a great sum of money, in fact, that your wife has to weigh it, and can afford to leave coins stuck to the pan." Kassim held out his hand and showed Ali Baba the coin. Ayesha squeaked. "You'd better tell me what's been going on," said Kassim. "And don't even think about lying."

Ali Baba sighed. Being good-hearted, he couldn't be cross with the wife he loved, and he didn't really mind giving the whole story to his brother. Kassim listened in silence, his eyes glittering with greed. Then he went home, determined to take all the treasure of the secret cave for himself.

95

"Oh well, never mind," said Ali Baba when Kassim had left. "I'd been thinking we should use the money anyway, not worry about it. Who'll notice if we spend some on the house, and buy a few new clothes for ourselves and Ahmed? We could even hire a servant girl to help with the housework…"

So the next morning, Ali Baba, Ayesha and Ahmed went shopping in the bazaar, then hired a girl called Marjanah to be their servant. Marjanah was an orphan who had grown up in poverty, and was very grateful for the job.

Meanwhile, an eager and excited Kassim was making his way through the forest with a train of donkeys to carry the hidden treasure home. Kassim arrived at last, and stood before the wall. He looked round to make sure he was completely alone, and cleared his throat. Then he said, "Open sesame!"

And the hidden door opened smoothly, just as it had done for Ali Baba.

Kassim gave a little giggle of delight, and went into the cave. He lit a torch he'd brought, and stared at the kind of sight guaranteed to make the heart of a greedy man beat faster. But there was no time to waste. He turned and said, "Close sesame!" – he didn't want any stray passers-by to discover the cave, or see what he was doing – and he started choosing what to take.

He soon had a great heap of bags and chests by the entrance, although by then his mind was fizzing with plans to return for the rest, and schemes for what he could do now he was probably the richest man in the world, and the sheer excitement of what was happening. He looked at the heap, decided he had just about enough donkeys to transport it, then turned to face the door.

He opened his mouth – and realised he had forgotten the magic words.

The truth was that Kassim's brain didn't have a great deal of room in it, and all the plans and schemes and excitement had pushed almost everything else out. He knew the first magic word was, "Open…" of course, that was obvious. And the second was a common seed, something you planted…

"OPEN… WHEAT!" he said, to no effect. "OPEN…CORN!" he shouted. "OPEN…BARLEY! OPEN…RICE! Er…OPEN…OH, FOR HEAVEN'S SAKE, JUST OPEN!" But the door stayed obstinately, infuriatingly shut.

Kassim pounded on the rock with his fists – and suddenly it opened! But his smile of relief soon vanished…for standing outside were the forty thieves, their captain at their head, and none of them looked too happy. The captain drew out his sword – it was a great, curved, wickedly sharp scimitar – and advanced into the cave, pushing Kassim in too. Kassim stumbled, and fell…

The bandits' suspicions had been aroused when they'd arrived at their secret cave to find a train of pack donkeys tethered outside. Now they were furious to discover someone was actually in it, and they didn't stop to ask questions. The captain killed Kassim, and savagely chopped his body into several pieces, which his men hung inside the entrance as a grisly warning.

Then they closed the cave door and galloped off down the forest path.

Night came, and Fatimah waited for her husband to return, her own mind filled with excitement at the prospect of the gold and jewels he had promised to bring her. But the hours passed with no sign of Kassim, and by the time the sun rose the next morning, Fatimah was frantic with worry. She ran to Ali Baba's house, and demanded that he go and find out what had happened.

Ali Baba set off with his donkey, filled with fear for his brother. And of course, he was horrified when the cave door opened and he saw the pieces of Kassim's body hanging inside the entrance. He quickly put them into a couple of empty sacks, loaded them on the donkey, and then – remembering to close the cave door behind him – he hurried home to Ayesha and Fatimah with the terrible news.

Fatimah wailed and tore her hair, and Ayesha tried to comfort her. Ali Baba, however, was brooding about the consequences of Kassim's death.

"We can't let anyone know he was chopped up," he said. "If the bandits hear, they'll be able to work out that I know about the secret cave, too. We'll just have to find some way of putting Kassim's body back together again before we let the undertakers see him. But I've no idea how."

"Can I make a suggestion?" said somebody. It was Marjanah, the servant girl, who had been listening. She had already grown to love her employers – and she wanted to help them now. "An old tailor lives on the other side of town," she went on, "and everyone says he's so good at his work that he could stitch a gash in your skin and leave no scar. Perhaps we could ask him to do it."

Ali Baba was impressed by Marjanah's cleverness, and so was Ahmed, who had come when he'd heard Fatimah wailing. In fact, the two young people rather liked the look of each other and – Ahmed was even more impressed when Marjanah came up with the plan for keeping things secret.

Marjanah went to see the tailor, and offered him a large payment for a special job. He agreed, and Marjanah led him blindfolded to the dark cellar of Ali Baba's house, where she took off his blindfold and showed him the pieces of Kassim. The tailor shrugged, thought of the money, did the job. Then the tailor was blindfolded again and taken back to his shop, where Marjanah thanked him, gave him a large bonus, and swore him to secrecy. Marjanah had been right – the tailor's work was so good you couldn't see the stitches. The next day Ali Baba sadly announced that his beloved brother Kassim had died in his sleep, and an expensive funeral was arranged. And afterwards, Ali Baba sighed with relief, and hoped that was the end of it. But alas, it wasn't. At that very moment the captain of the bandits was swearing, and kicking at the treasure heaps in the secret cave. As soon as the cave door had opened and he'd seen that the pieces of Kassim's body had gone, he realized that somebody else must know the secret of the hidden cave.

"We must find whoever it is and kill him!" he roared.

"Yes, and all his family!" roared his thirty-nine men.

And so the captain and his men went into the city in disguise. They asked – casually, discreetly, trying not to arouse any suspicion – if there had been a recent funeral involving a corpse chopped into several pieces. They had no luck – but then one of the bandits happened to stop at the tailor's shop…

By now the tailor had had time to think about what he'd done, and he was finding it very hard to keep to his vow of secrecy. It didn't take the bandit long to get the truth out of him, and then – after a small payment was offered and accepted – the tailor allowed himself to be blindfolded once more. He led the bandit to Ali Baba's house by touch and hearing and smell. The bandit smiled, and marked the doorpost with a small chalk cross. Then he quickly took the tailor back to his shop, and hurried off to find the captain.

A while later, Marjanah came back from shopping in the bazaar, and noticed the chalk cross. It immediately made her feel uneasy, so she found some chalk and made crosses on the other doorposts in the street. She didn't mention the incident to Ali Baba, not wanting to worry him or the rest of the family – Fatimah was living with them now, and in a very fragile state – but Marjanah decided she would definitely stay alert from that moment on.

The captain, however, wasn't so easily fooled. When he saw the crosses on every door, he marched off to the tailor's shop. Soon the happy tailor – he'd been given yet another payment of gold coins – was blindfolded again and led the captain back to Ali Baba's house. The captain didn't mark the doorpost, though – he knew he'd remember the house well enough without that…

The next evening, there was a knocking on Ali Baba's front door. He went to open it, and found himself facing a man whose face was half covered by his turban. Behind the man was a line of packhorses, each one bearing a large earthenware jar.

"Good evening, friend," said the man. "I am a travelling merchant, just arrived in your city, and I wondered if you might know of a place to stay."

"Why, you must stay here!" replied Ali Baba, as generous as ever, of course. "Your packhorses will be safe in the courtyard behind the house…"

The man smiled wickedly as Ali Baba led him in. The plan was going smoothly – for this was none other than the captain in disguise. He had made inquiries about the man who lived in this house, and been told of his kind-heartedness, so he'd guessed Ali Baba would offer him a bed for the night.

But the captain wouldn't be staying in bed. Each of those earthenware jars concealed one of the captain's men, and they were waiting for his signal – a light tap on the outside of the jar – to creep out and slaughter every living thing in the house. And then the secret of the cave would be safe again.

Ali Baba insisted on giving his guest a meal before bedtime. Marjanah prepared it for him, then went out to check that the horses were comfortable. She'd heard Ali Baba asking the merchant what was in the jars, and the man had said they were filled with olive oil.

Marjanah accidentally brushed against one of the jars, and froze when she heard a man's voice whisper from within it.

"Is it time yet?" said the voice. Suddenly Marjanah suspected that her master and his family were in mortal danger. She realised that the merchant must be the captain of the bandits, and that his men were concealed in the jars.

"Not yet," she whispered back, thinking quickly. She went round the other jars, tapping on them all. From each one somebody asked the same question – "Is it time yet?" and Marjanah gave them the same answer. Then she went indoors and came up with yet another plan.

Marjanah boiled up a great quantity of oil – and poured it into each of the jars, killing all thirty-nine bandits. She went to tell Ali Baba, and just then the captain went to the courtyard to summon his men. But he soon found out they were all dead – and he realised that his plot had been uncovered. So he panicked, and fled into the night before he too was killed. But he vowed to wreak his revenge…

Ali Baba didn't believe Marjanah at first, but when she showed him the bodies in the jars and they discovered that the merchant had gone, he went cold at the thought of what might have happened to him and his family.

"I can't ever thank you enough, Marjanah," Ali Baba murmured. "And I can't help feeling that I don't deserve such devoted service as yours…"

"Oh, but you do!" said Marjanah. "I'd do anything to help you – no one I've ever met has been as kind and generous to me as you and Ayesha!"

"It's nice of you to say so," Ali Baba replied shyly. "But I hope you won't have to do anything that dramatic again. Maybe this really is the end of it."

Things did seem to quieten down over the next few weeks and months, so Ali Baba and his family relaxed and enjoyed their prosperity. Ali Baba set up a woodcutting business, hiring other men to do what he had always done, and paying them fairly. Soon he began to grow wealthy – wealthy enough to set Ahmed up in business with a shop of his own. Ahmed worked hard, and before long he was wealthy too.

Then one day, several years later, Ahmed asked Ali Baba if he could invite a friend of his to dinner at their house.

"His name is Hussein," said Ahmed, "and he owns the shop next door to mine. He's been a real help, and I'd like to thank him for all he's done."

Ali Baba agreed straightaway, and the feast was arranged. All the family were there – Ali Baba, Ayesha, Ahmed, even Fatimah – and the guest of honour arrived bang on time.

Marjanah took Hussein's cloak to hang it up, and watched him. After all this time she had begun to think that they must be safe. But there was something about this man that made her feel uneasy. So she decided to keep a close eye on him.

She served the food, then went round with a flask of wine. Hussein was laughing and joking and being friendly, and for a second Marjanah thought she was worrying too much. Then she leaned over him to pour some wine into his cup, and glimpsed something that chilled her blood.

The handle of a dagger was concealed inside Hussein's tunic.

Marjanah instantly realised why Hussein was familiar – he was disguised again, but she knew now that he was the merchant whose men she had killed in the jars. Which meant he was also the captain of the bandits, and had come to kill Ali Baba and the rest of the family…and her too!

Marjanah didn't say anything – but she slipped into the kitchen and grabbed a knife, which she kept behind her back when she returned to the feast. And she was just in time. For Ali Baba had turned away from Hussein to say something to Ahmed, and Hussein had his hand inside his tunic…

Marjanah strode over and plunged her knife into Hussein's heart.

Hussein died instantly – and then there was chaos. Ayesha and Fatimah screamed – Fatimah screamed the loudest, of course – while both Ali Baba and Ahmed leapt to their feet with expressions of horror on both their faces.

"But why have you have killed my friend?" wailed Ahmed.

"Yes, why?" said Ali Baba. "Are you completely mad, girl?"

"No, I'm not," said Marjanah. "He was about to kill you!"

Marjanah explained everything, and as soon as Ali Baba saw the dagger concealed in Hussein's tunic, he realised she was telling the truth. And when he looked more closely at Hussein, he wondered why he hadn't seen that this supposed friend of Ahmed's was none other than the captain of the bandits…

And so they were safe – and here the exciting, dangerous part of the story comes to an end, although many other good things happened later, among them a wedding. To Ali Baba's delight, Marjanah and Ahmed announced that they were in love and wanted to get married, which they soon did.

And Ali Baba and his family lived in happiness and prosperity ever after, their growing wealth helped by occasional visits to a certain hidden cave.

They were the only ones who knew about it, after all…

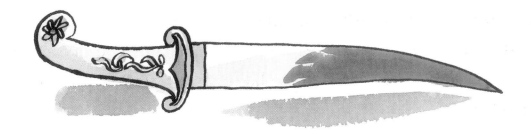

THE MAN-EATING MONSTER
THE STORY OF THESEUS & THE MINOTAUR

THERE HAVE BEEN FEW VILLAINS AS EVIL or bloodthirsty as Minos, king of the island of Crete. Every ruler in the lands of the eastern Mediterranean feared him. He had fleets of mighty warships, and more warriors than you could count. But worst of all, he had a terrifying monster called the Minotaur.

This creature was half-man and half-bull, and some said it was three times the size of either, with huge horns and a hunger for human flesh. Minos kept the beast in a maze called the Labyrinth, and fed it on young boys and girls that he forced the other rulers to send to him. None of them dared refuse.

To the north of Crete lay the kingdom of Athens, whose ruler was Aegeus. Every year, Aegeus' son, Theseus, watched as a black-sailed ship from Crete arrived. He watched as seven boys and seven girls were chosen to be fed to the Minotaur. He watched as they were dragged from their sobbing parents and put in Cretan chains.

Then one year he decided that he could watch no more.

"Wait!" he yelled, and stepped forward. "Take me...I'll go!"

The crowd gasped, and Aegeus tried to hold back his son. "This is utter madness," said Aegeus. "I won't allow it!"

"I'm sorry, Father," said Theseus, "but I must go. I intend to kill the Minotaur, and put a stop to this awful nightmare once and for all."

Aegeus was proud of his son's courage, but appalled by his foolhardiness, and tried desperately to argue with him. But Theseus had made his mind up, and Aegeus finally gave in. The Cretans smirked as they grabbed the prince and chained him to the others. Soon their sleek ship was heading out to sea.

"I'll keep watch from the cliffs for your return!" shouted Aegeus, the tears streaming down his face. "Make sure you raise a white sail as a signal that you're safe. If it's black, then I'll know the worst has happened..."

"I will, Father!" shouted Theseus. "I promise!"

When they arrived at last in Crete, Theseus and the others were taken straight to King Minos. The king sat on the great throne in his magnificent palace, and laughed when the soldiers told him what Theseus had said.

"So…Aegeus has sent me a real hero this year," sneered King Minos, looking the young prince up and down. "What makes you think you can kill my monster? And how are you going to do it? With your bare hands?"

"If I have to," said Theseus defiantly, his head held high, even though he was beginning to feel a little nervous. The king's daughter Ariadne was watching Theseus closely, but all she saw was his pride and bravery. Ariadne was afraid of her father, and hated him too.

A plan formed in her mind.

"Well then, I think we've got something to look forward to," said King Minos. "I'm sure the Minotaur will find you rather more entertaining than his usual meals. Guards, take them away! The fun begins tomorrow!"

The boys and girls from Athens were locked up in a dungeon for the night. The others were terrified, and Theseus tried to comfort them. But he was scared too, and regretted getting himself into such a tight spot. How could he possibly kill a savage beast like the Minotaur all by himself?

Suddenly Theseus heard somebody softly whispering his name.

He crept over to the dungeon door, where a girl was looking at him through the bars.

"I'm Ariadne, daughter of King Minos," she said, producing a key and unlocking the door to let Theseus out, "and I have an offer for you. If you do what I ask, then I will help you kill the Minotaur and escape from Crete."

"What exactly do you want?" said Theseus, wondering if this was some kind of trick. He didn't trust King Minos.

"Just that you take me with you," said Ariadne. "Oh…and marry me."

Theseus was surprised by Ariadne's second condition, and didn't like the idea very much. But all that mattered was that he should kill the Minotaur. He would worry about anything else afterwards.

"Very well," he said, crossing his fingers behind his back. "I agree."

So Ariadne led Theseus from the darkened palace, taking a flaming torch to light their way. Nobody saw them – she had slipped the guards a potion to make them sleep. Ariadne and Theseus crept down a path until they reached a wall of rock with a black, forbidding hole in it, like the entrance to a tomb.

Theseus' mouth was dry, and he could feel his heart beating fast.

"The Labyrinth is huge, its endless tunnels darker than my father's soul," whispered Ariadne, "and anyone who ventures inside is soon lost. The monster knows every nook and cranny, and will track you down wherever you are. But with this magic ball of thread, you can find him first."

All they had to do was tie the loose end of the thread to a bush near

110

the entrance, and drop the ball on the ground. The thread would unroll, seeking the Minotaur, and Theseus could follow it. Should he survive his encounter with the beast, he could find his way out by rolling up the thread again.

"But how do I kill the Minotaur?" said Theseus. "I know I said I'd use my bare hands if I had to, but I'd rather have a weapon, even if only a knife."

"I've thought of that too," said Ariadne, pulling something from a hiding place behind another bush. "Here, take this," she said, "and use it well."

It was a beautiful sword, its razor-sharp edge glinting in the torchlight.

Ariadne gave Theseus the sword and the torch, and tied one end of the thread to a bush. Then she dropped the magic ball on the ground, and it bounced off, into the entrance of the Labyrinth. Theseus took a deep breath…then followed it. Strange, scary shadows flickered ahead of him.

He needed all his courage to keep going. His heart was pounding, and every time he came to a bend in a tunnel, he wondered if the monster might be waiting beyond it. He saw nothing, though, and the only sounds were his own breathing and the scuffing of his sandals on the gritty tunnel floor.

At last the ball of thread was completely unwound, and Theseus found himself standing in the centre of the Labyrinth, his torch barely illuminating a vast chamber. Before him lay a scattering of broken, bloody, chewed-on human bones – the gory remains of the Minotaur's many previous victims.

Suddenly a giant, menacing figure rose in the shadows and advanced, making the floor shake. Theseus' heart nearly leapt from his chest as he saw a pair of huge horns gleaming white, and his torchlight reflected in a pair of evil eyes. The Minotaur was twice, no, three, four, five times his size.

"Who dares trespass in the Minotaur's lair?" boomed a colossal voice.

"Theseus of Athens, son of King Aegeus," replied the young hero, his whole body trembling, his own voice unsteady. "Prepare to die, foul beast!"

It was now or never, thought Theseus. So he yelled his loudest war cry and charged the Minotaur, torch in one hand, sword raised in the other. The monster roared, and bellowed, and tried to crush him to death under its giant hooves. Theseus swung, and swiped, and danced nimbly out of its reach.

But it was hard and terrifying work, and Theseus knew he couldn't keep it up for long. Then, just when he thought he couldn't stay clear of the beast's reach any more, he felt his blade bite into the back of the Minotaur's leg. The monster fell backwards with a stupendous crash, screaming with rage and pain. Theseus quickly leapt forward and plunged his sword into the monster's chest, killing the beast instantly. Then he pulled his blade out, wiped it clean of blood on the Minotaur's rough hide, and paused to get his breath before he started rolling up the thread again. He could barely believe he'd survived.

Ariadne was waiting for him when he emerged from the Labyrinth.

"Come on," she said. "We don't have much time!"

They returned to the palace, and Theseus quickly freed the other boys and girls. Then Ariadne led them silently down to the harbour. A Cretan warrior saw them and raised the alarm, and more warriors chased them. But Theseus found a ship, and the Athenians made their escape under a hail of arrows. There isn't much more to tell –

except to say that Theseus didn't keep his promise to marry Ariadne. He took her with him, but the more he thought about it, the less he wanted to marry her.

He forgot that without her help he couldn't have killed the Minotaur. After all, what kind of girl is it who knows how to make sleeping potions and is happy to betray her own father?

So when they stopped at an island for water, Theseus left Ariadne behind, and never looked back. Some say she stayed marooned till she died, others that she went home and made peace with her father, still others that one of the gods took her as his wife. Whatever the truth, her story ends here.

And Theseus broke his promise to his father, too. The Cretan ship had a black sail, and Theseus forgot to change it for a white one. When King Aegeus saw the black sail he had been dreading, he thought the worst. He threw himself into the sea and drowned, believing his son had been eaten by the Minotaur.

Theseus was heartbroken. But from then on, life was better for the people of Athens. King Minos was far too scared of the hero who had killed the Minotaur to threaten them ever again. And Theseus never forgot his father.

Indeed, he decided to name the sea between Athens and Crete after him.

We call it the Aegean Sea to this day.

THE SILVER ARROW

THE STORY OF ROBIN HOOD & THE SHERIFF

TIMES WERE TOUGH IN ENGLAND IN THE YEARS after the Norman invaders came. They conquered the whole country with fire and sword, they robbed and killed and looted and pillaged, and they took the best of everything for themselves, especially the farmland. Then they settled down to rule over the ordinary people – the Saxons – with violence and cruelty and scorn.

Few dared stand against their might, and those that did rebel were soon crushed, all except one…a young man the people knew as Robin Hood.

Some said that Robin was really Robert of Locksley, the son of a Saxon noble, and that his father had been murdered by some Norman knights so they could seize his land. Others said Robin was the son of a poor hunter, or a yeoman farmer's son who had been set upon by a gang of Norman soldiers for no reason – and had left three of them dead before making his escape.

Whatever the truth, Robin had long ago been declared an outlaw, and had taken refuge in the depths of Sherwood Forest, an ancient wood that stood near the city of Nottingham. There he gathered a band of faithful followers – boys and men, and some girls and women too – many of whom had seen their homes burned and their entire families slaughtered before their eyes.

But Robin and his followers – his band of outlaws, as he called them – did a lot more than just hide. They struck back, hard and often, swooping on columns of Norman soldiers who strayed near the forest, killing dozens in a hail of arrows, then silently returning into the darkness between the trees. They held up Norman travellers as well, robbing the rich to give to the poor.

The Saxons adored Robin, and wherever the people gathered they told each other news of his latest escapades. They were proud of his daring and his boldness, his sense of humour and his fighting skills – many of the outlaws were fine archers, Will Scarlett being particularly good – but Robin was said to be the best shot with a longbow in England. And somehow just knowing Robin was standing up for them seemed to keep the people going.

The Normans, of course, feared and hated Robin Hood in equal measure.

One Norman in particular – the Sheriff of Nottingham, the local overlord, a brutal and cunning man – grew ever more determined to catch Robin and end his mischief once and for all. But no matter how many expeditions he sent against Robin, no matter how many men he set to guard travellers on the road, he could no more catch Robin Hood than seize a handful of mist.

So the sheriff brooded in his great grim stone castle, wondering what he could do. And eventually he devised a plan that he thought might work.

One dark evening, a young boy – the son of one of the outlaws – ran into a clearing deep in the heart of Sherwood Forest, the secret hideaway of Robin and his band. They were sitting round a campfire, eating their evening meal – venison from a deer that belonged to the Sheriff of Nottingham. Robin always said poaching deer from the sheriff made it taste even better.

"Robin!" said the boy, skidding to a halt before him. "Have a look at this! It was pinned to the door of a tavern, and there are more all over the place!"

The boy eagerly held out a piece of parchment to Robin, who took it from him and read what was written on it. Then Robin smiled, and looked up.

"Listen to this, lads," he said, and the outlaws grew quiet. "It seems our old friend the Sheriff of Nottingham is in need of entertainment – he wants to find the best bowman in England, so he's holding an archery contest at the castle. There's a rich prize for the man who wins, too – a silver arrow."

"But…you're not seriously thinking of entering, are you, Robin?" said Marian, Robin's sweetheart, a worried expression on her face. "It's a trap."

"Marian's right, Robin," said Will Scarlett, who'd been with him since the earliest days in Sherwood. "He knows you're the best archer in England…"

"And he knows you can't resist a challenge," said Friar Tuck, another longstanding band member. "So it's just a crafty way of flushing you out."

One by one, the other outlaws – Much the Miller's son, Little John, Alan A'Dale and the rest – joined in, each of them saying the same thing, all of them worried for their leader. The clearing was filled with the noise of their voices, until at last Robin held up his hands and quietened them down again.

"Of course it's a trap," said Robin, still smiling in the flickering firelight. "I know that as well as any of you. All the more reason to go – and beat it."

"But what good will it do to put yourself in such danger?" said Marian. "You're the people's only hope, the only thing that keeps them going…"

"Exactly!" said Robin, grinning now. "So think how they'll feel if I can beat the sheriff at his own game, if I can tweak his beard in front of them!"

"Ah, since you put it like that…" murmured Friar Tuck, eyes twinkling. The other outlaws were glancing at each other, several of them starting to smile too. Marian, however, looked as if she needed more convincing.

"I'm not sure, Robin," she said, frowning at him. "I think it's too risky."

"For heaven's sake, Marian, just being a Saxon these days is pretty risky!" laughed Robin. The outlaws laughed with him, and Marian smiled. "At least this way we might have some fun," Robin added. "Anyway, trust me – I'll come up with a plan. The sheriff isn't the only one who can be cunning…"

A week later, the day of the archery contest dawned bright and sunny, and a great crowd began to gather in the main courtyard

of the sheriff's castle. The Saxon people – who needed some entertainment themselves – were kept to one side, penned in behind a barrier, and watched by a line of hard-faced Norman soldiers in their iron helmets and chain-mail – their swords drawn.

A special pavilion – a gaudy thing of bright silks and fluttering pennants – had been set up for the sheriff at the far end of the courtyard, so he could have the best view of the contest, and also be protected from the glare of the sun. He sat in a chair as big as a king's throne, on a raised platform flanked by his bodyguard, and surrounded by rich, local Normans and their wives.

A low table stood in front of the sheriff, and the silver arrow lay on it.

"I trust our men have been told to stay vigilant," the sheriff muttered to the captain of the guard, who was standing beside him. "And that they're to ensure – on pain of their own deaths – that the man we want doesn't escape."

"Don't worry, my lord, they've all been fully briefed," the captain replied, smiling. "This is going to be a day to remember! By the way, two of the guard have said they want to enter the contest themselves. Do they have your permission?"

"Yes, yes," the sheriff hissed irritably, and waved the captain away.

The sheriff, in fact, was feeling rather tense, and kept scanning the faces in the crowd, wondering if one of them might be his arch-enemy, the shadowy Saxon outlaw who had caused him so much trouble. The sheriff had never seen Robin Hood, so he had no idea what he looked like. No one had even been able to give the sheriff a description of him.

At last the sheriff summoned his herald and told him to get things moving. The herald blew his trumpet, and the competitors marched out.

They lined up before the sheriff, and the herald explained the rules of the contest. The sheriff leaned forward to study the competitors more closely, knowing already that more than a hundred men from all over the country had come to try and win the silver arrow. He could see now that they were mostly Saxons, some young, a few old, the rest of them ordinary-looking Saxon peasants, except for the two Normans the captain had mentioned, who stood apart.

Only one of the contestants seemed to stand out, the sheriff thought, and that was a sturdy fellow, dressed from head to foot in Lincoln green – and with the hood of his tunic raised so no one could see his face. "Umm, very suspicious," thought the sheriff, narrowing his eyes and rubbing his chin. He decided this mysterious, hooded archer might well be the man to watch.

Then, with another blast from the herald's trumpet, the contest began.

The targets had been set up against the castle wall, at a distance of fifty paces for the first round.

The archers stepped forward, one by one, to take their shots, the crowd loudly enjoying themselves, the sheriff and his men silently watching the proceedings like hawks.

Half the competitors were quickly eliminated, the targets moved back a further twenty-five paces, and so on.

Soon there were ten competitors, the target at a hundred and twenty-five paces, then five archers with the target at a hundred and fifty paces, and all five were very good. Two of them were the Norman soldiers who had entered the contest, which gave the sheriff some satisfaction – at least it showed the Saxons that Normans could be good archers too, although the crowd booed every time they took a shot.

The other three were Saxons, two of them fine archers, but the third had easily been the best bowman of all during the contest so far – and he was none other than the mysterious hooded man. He hit the centre of the target every time, and never lowered his hood or seemed to speak.

The sheriff glanced now at the captain of his bodyguard, and nodded slightly at him.

The captain turned to whisper an order to one of his men, and soon more Norman soldiers appeared from behind the pavilion. They moved forward and stood behind the five competitors, the bright sunlight glinting off their iron helmets and their swords. The captain looked at the sheriff, but the sheriff gave him a signal that obviously meant he should wait a little…

Meanwhile, the contest was entering its final phase. The two Saxons took their last shots, which were fine, but not good enough to win. Then the two Normans took their shots, which were of much the same standard. And then the mysterious, hooded man stepped forward. A hush fell over the castle courtyard, everyone holding their breath as he raised his great longbow.

He pulled back the string, aimed – and let fly, the arrow swishing through the air and THUDDING into the dead centre of the target, the best shot of the day. The Saxon crowd cheered happily…but then things happened fast.

"Hold that man!" yelled the sheriff, who could remain patient no longer.

The waiting soldiers did just that, grabbing the mysterious hooded man and holding him by the arms. The crowd murmured in confusion, then began to boo, but the sheriff took no notice. He leapt up from his seat and strode over to the soldiers and the contestants, the captain hurrying behind him.

"My lord," the captain said breathlessly, "I think you should know that –

"Not now, you idiot!" the sheriff snapped, irritably waving him away again. The sheriff walked on, stopping eventually in front of the hooded man, who stood between his Norman captors with his head down.

"So, Robin Hood," he said, practically spitting out the name, "we meet at last." And with that the sheriff roughly pulled back the man's hood to reveal a smiling young face. "Well, what do you have to say?" snarled the sheriff.

"Not much," said the young man. "Except that I am not the one you seek."

"Hah!" snorted the sheriff. "You're just trying to save your skin. Guards, take the wretch away. We'll hang him later – after we've tortured him…"

"Not so fast there, lads!" said one of the two Norman soldiers who had competed in the contest. "He's telling the truth. He isn't Robin Hood."

"What are you talking about, man?" the sheriff spluttered furiously, his face red with anger. "How can you possibly know whether he is or he isn't?"

"Because his name is Will Scarlett," said the soldier, removing his helmet. "I am Robin Hood. And now it's time to end this contest. Seize him, Alan!"

Suddenly the other Norman contestant whipped out a dagger and moved forward. And before anyone could stop him, he grabbed the sheriff and held the dagger to his throat, the point pressing into the skin. The crowd howled, and the sheriff's men were dazed and confused, not knowing what to do.

"Don't just stand there, you fools!" the sheriff yelled. "Kill them!"

"I wouldn't do that, if I were you, lads," said Robin, and smiled at them. "One false move, and I promise you that my friend Alan here will cut the sheriff a brand new windpipe. In fact, you'd better all drop your weapons. And if you want another reason for doing that, have a look around you!"

The captain and his men did as Robin said, and saw figures suddenly appearing on the castle walls and emerging from the crowd – outlaws from Robin's band, each one carrying a bow with an arrow aimed at a Norman heart. Several of the contestants stepped forward and joined Robin too.

The captain and his men dropped their weapons with a clatter.

"I'm very sorry, my lord," said the captain. "But I was trying to tell you, we found a couple of the men stripped of their uniforms and tied up…"

"All part of the plan, Sheriff," said Robin. "And not a bad fit, either." Then Robin turned to address the crowd. "The sheriff thought he could trap me, Robin Hood, by setting up this contest," he said, his voice ringing loud and clear. "But it looks like we've managed to spoil his day, don't you think?"

The crowd roared its appreciation, and Robin and his outlaws smiled.

"Bah!" snorted the sheriff. "If you are Robin Hood, then the stories about your archery can't be true. You were beaten in the contest fair and square."

"Is that so?" said Robin. He knew the sheriff was trying to belittle him in front of the crowd. "Well, perhaps I'd better give everybody here a taste of what I can really do. You don't mind if I have another shot, do you, Will?"

"Be my guest, Robin," said Will. "But mine is a hard shot to beat."

Robin didn't reply. He raised his bow, took an arrow from his quiver and fitted it to the string. He slowly drew the arrow back until its tail feathers rested on his cheek. He aimed at the target, the one with Will's last arrow still sticking out of its centre. And once more the crowd – in fact everybody in the courtyard, Norman and Saxon, rich and poor alike – held its breath.

Robin stood for several seconds, bow poised, the sun shining on him.

Then he released the string, and his arrow flew straight and true through the air…and split Will's arrow right down the middle, THWACKING into exactly the same spot at the very centre of the target. A great cheer went up from the crowd, and even the Normans were impressed, the sheriff's jaw falling open in amazement against Alan A'Dale's arm round his throat.

"Well, that ought to prove who I am, and no mistake," said Robin. "And I think a shot like that deserves a rich prize – don't you, Sheriff? Will, fetch me that silver arrow while I find out where Marian's got to with the horses."

Will went to collect the silver arrow from where it lay on the table in front of the pavilion, and Robin pulled a hunting horn from beneath his chainmail. He blew three loud blasts on it, and soon Marian came cantering through the castle gates on a tall horse, leading four more behind her, and rode up to him. She was wearing Lincoln green and had a bow slung across her back.

"I take it everything's gone to plan then, Robin?" she said, and smiled.

"Oh yes, Marian," Robin replied, swinging into the saddle of one of the spare horses. "And now it's time to head for home. I'm afraid you're coming too, Sheriff," he added. "At least as far as the edge of the forest, anyway. But it's a lovely day for a ride in the country, so I'm sure you'll enjoy it."

Will got the sheriff on to one of the horses and tied his hands to the saddle. Then they mounted, and Robin led them past the cheering crowd and towards the gate, holding the silver arrow above his head in triumph, Marian beside him. Once outside, they broke into a gallop, hooves thundering as they made for Sherwood Forest in the distance.

And inside the castle, the other outlaws faded away like ghosts in the sunlight before the Normans managed to pull themselves together and do anything…

A few hours later the sheriff returned, still tied to a horse, but sitting backwards on it now, and minus all his clothes. The Saxon people thought it was the funniest thing they'd ever seen, and the story soon travelled round England, along with the tale of everything else that had happened that day.

Robin's fight against the Normans wasn't over, of course. It went on for many more years, and he and the Sheriff of Nottingham had other encounters, although the sheriff's reputation never recovered. Robin's fame grew and grew, though, and to this day, wherever poor people fight against tyranny, his name is remembered and the stories about him told.

But this story's at an end. So let's leave Robin and his band of outlaws, sitting round their campfire surrounded by the dark of Sherwood Forest, the sound of their talk and laughter rising to the branches above their heads.